South Africa

J F AYLETT

Contents

Chapter 1	Sowing the Seeds of Fear and Hatred	2
Chapter 2	The Boers in Control	4
Chapter 3	A Word about Race	6
Chapter 4	Apartheid	8
Chapter 5	The African National Congress	14
Chapter 6	Massacre at Sharpeville (1960)	16
Chapter 7	Nelson Mandela	20
Chapter 8	Bantustans	22
Chapter 9	Foreign Affairs	24
Chapter 10	The 1970s	26
Chapter 11	The 1980s	32
Chapter 12	The End of Apartheid	38
Chapter 13	After Apartheid	46
Afterword and Glossary		48
Index		Inside back cover

HODDER 20th CENTURY *History*

HODDER
EDUCATION
AN HACHETTE UK COMPANY

Sowing the Seeds of Fear and Hate

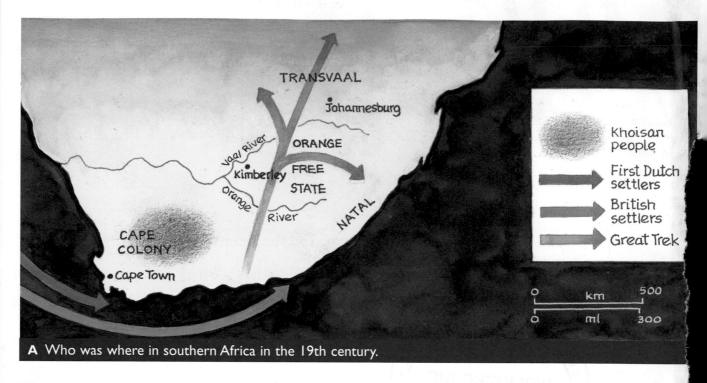

A Who was where in southern Africa in the 19th century.

The first white settlers arrived at the Cape of Good Hope in 1652. They were traders working for the Dutch East India Company. Twenty years later, they bought the area from a local chief for £800. From early on, these settlers looked for the best farmland. They took it from the black tribespeople who already lived there. The settlers called them Hottentots and Bushmen. Today, they are known as the Khoi-san.

The settlers also needed workers on their new land. The black people who had lost it were forced to become labourers for the whites. Others were driven away or shot on hunting expeditions, like animals. From 1658 onwards, the Dutch also imported black slaves, mostly from West Africa.

The settlement was never very large. In the first 50 years, only about 2500 white people arrived. Half of these were Dutch but there were people from other countries, including French refugees.

In 1707, the Dutch company stopped all **immigration**; for over 100 years, no new immigrants arrived. During this time, the settlers had little contact with Europe. Their ways of thinking were similar to those of the early settlers. Major events and new ideas mostly passed them by.

This ended abruptly in 1806 when the British captured the Cape. In 1814, Britain bought the Cape from the Dutch and it became part of the growing British Empire.

This started a new wave of conflict: white people against white people. The settlers called themselves Boers (meaning farmers) or Afrikaners (meaning Africans). They did not want to be ruled by the British; they disliked the British interfering in their lives. For instance, they objected when the British introduced a black police force: the Boers thought that black people were inferior.

They were furious when Britain banned slavery in its empire in 1833. The Boers did not believe that black and white people were equal. So they decided to move away to become independent once more. They packed their possessions and families into great ox wagons and drove north-wards. From 1835 onwards, thousands made this journey. It became known as the 'Great Trek'.

These journeys led to fierce battles with the Zulus, the strongest of the black tribes living in this area. Many of the Boers settled on Zulu land, which they called Natal. However, in 1845, the British made Natal into a British colony. So most of the Boers set off again.

Eventually, they crossed the Orange River and set up two new states for themselves – Orange Free State and the Transvaal. This was land that the black tribes believed was theirs. However, the Boers were now free of the British – but not for long.

The peace did not last for long. In 1866, some children playing beside the river at Kimberley found a bright pebble. A year later, it was identified as a diamond and a gold rush began. Thousands of white prospectors turned up, hoping to make their fortune. So did even more black people, looking for work.

These black workers were herded into compounds. This system kept costs down and made it easier to control the workforce. If black workers wanted to go into town, they had to get a pass from the whites.

In 1871, the British took over the diamond fields on the grounds that such large numbers of people needed controlling. In 1877, they took control of the Transvaal, too.

This created a new problem. The British now had to support the Boers against the Zulus in their struggle for land. The Zulu king, Cetshwayo, refused to give up his own kingdom or his army which defended it. A bitter war followed but the British eventually won. The Zulu kingdom was carved up into areas, each ruled by a Zulu chief. It was added to the British Empire.

By now, the Boers did not trust the British at all. The situation grew worse after 1886, when gold was discovered at Witwatersrand in the heart of the Transvaal. British prospectors flooded into the area and a town called Johannesburg grew up.

The Boers were soon outnumbered by these 'foreigners'. They worried that they would lose control of their republic. If these newcomers took over the country, the Boers could not flee north, as they had before. This time, they would have to fight.

In 1899, war broke out between the British and the Boers. The British called it the Boer War and the Boers called it the English War. The British expected a quick victory but it took three years before they forced the Boers to surrender. In the meantime, British soldiers burned Boer farms; they also moved Boer women and children into **concentration camps** to stop them helping the enemy.

Conditions in the camps were so bad that 26 000 women and children died. The Boers never forgave the British for this. Decades later, they still told stories of how the British had put powdered glass into the porridge to kill their families.

The British won the war. In 1902, they signed the Treaty of Vereeniging with the Boers. The Orange Free State and the Transvaal came under British rule. In return, the British paid the Boers £3 million and promised them that they would eventually be allowed to govern themselves.

The British kept their promise. In 1909, Britain created the dominion of South Africa. A dominion was a member of the British Empire which was mostly independent. This new dominion included four colonies – Transvaal and the Orange Free State, controlled by the Boers, and Natal and Cape Colony, controlled by the British. In other words, Britain handed over power to the white settlers.

The Boers were pleased with this solution. They now lived in a country which was mostly free of Britain. Also, they outnumbered the British in the new South Africa. They would hold all the key posts; they would run things their own way.

So South Africa was built on distrust and fear. The British did not trust the Boers and the Boers did not trust the British. Both groups feared the blacks and the blacks had good reason to fear the Boers. Blacks had few rights in the two Boer republics. There was no reason to suppose that they would be any better off in the new Union of South Africa. And so it turned out to be.

> 'The white man must rule' – British High Commissioner, 1897

B This French cartoon showed a Boer woman and dead children in a British concentration camp (1901–2).

Q

1 Draw a timeline to show events in southern Africa from 1806 to 1909.
2 a) Why did the Boers not trust the British?
   b) Why did the blacks not trust the Boers?
   c) Why did the British not trust the Boers?
3 How do you think the Boers will treat the blacks, now that they are in charge? Jot down your ideas and compare them.

The Boers in Control

Before the South Africa Act was passed, the colonies had to decide how to elect their MPs. Cape Colony had a voting system in which all races could vote. The Boers in the Transvaal and the Orange Free State had no intention of allowing non-Europeans to vote.

The result was a compromise: non-whites kept their vote in Cape Colony but were not allowed to stand for parliament. In theory, non-Europeans could vote in Natal but few ever did. Elsewhere, only whites were given the vote.

The Boers agreed on something else. White and black people should live separately, although black people would be needed to work on white farms and in white-owned industries. Many British in South Africa supported this policy.

In 1913, the new South African government put this policy into practice. The Natives Land Act allocated just 7.3 per cent of South African land to the blacks. White people would not be allowed to live on this land.

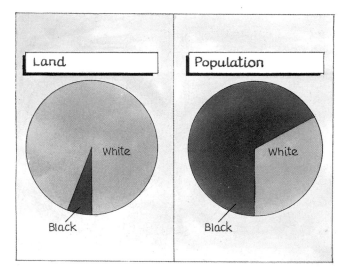

The total population at the time was about six million. Of these, about 4 million were black. They would not be allowed to live outside their **reservations;** they could not purchase land elsewhere. The rest of the land (92.7 per cent) was for the use of white people only.

The land allowed for the blacks could not provide work or food for all of them. Some reserves were so overcrowded that each person's share was little more than a garden. But this was what the white government intended. This law made sure that black people would have to work for white people to earn a living. So it guaranteed cheap labour for farmers and mine-owners.

A From a South African commission report (1922).

> The native should only be allowed to enter urban areas when he is willing to enter and *minister* to the White man. [He] should depart when he ceases to minister.

Protecting the whites

After 1924, South Africa was run by a **coalition** government, led by General Hertzog. He had fought against the British in the Boer War. Nevertheless, his Afrikaner National Party joined up with the Labour Party, which was mainly English-speaking. But the Afrikaners had the upper hand.

Hertzog wanted Afrikaners and British to work together but he also wanted to protect the Afrikaners' way of life. The new South Africa had two official languages: Dutch and English. But few Afrikaners spoke Dutch any more. They spoke Afrikaans, which had developed from Dutch. (In 1925, Afrikaans became an official language).

Hertzog believed in **white supremacy** and wanted to protect whites against any threat of black power in jobs or politics. He was determined to look after the interests of the poor white workers in South Africa. So, in 1926, his government passed a law which stopped blacks and Asians from doing skilled and semi-skilled jobs in the mines.

People called it the 'Colour Bar Act' because it made sure that only white people could do better-paid mine work. Black workers did basic mining jobs for poor pay. By 1943, a black miner was earning only £2.95 per month. This was the same wage that black miners had earned back in 1926. White miners earned more than ten times as much.

B This photograph showing conditions in a township was taken in 1921.

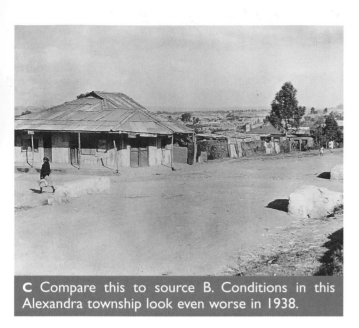

C Compare this to source B. Conditions in this Alexandra township look even worse in 1938.

In 1925, the government began forcing every black male aged 18–65 to pay a poll tax. In order to earn this money, blacks were forced to work for whites. This was what the politicians wanted.

Despite these laws, there were still many poor whites. Most Afrikaners were poor and competed with blacks to get jobs. By the early 1930s, more than 20 per cent of Afrikaners had sunk to a level which was thought fit only for blacks.

Keeping the whites white

Hertzog did not just want to preserve Afrikaners' culture; he wanted to preserve their race. In 1927, the Immorality Act banned any sexual intercourse between whites and blacks.

D Jan Smuts, South African Prime Minister, 1919-24, said:

It is dishonourable to mix black and white blood.

In 1933, the National Party joined up with the South Africa Party to work together to beat the depression. But a handful of Afrikaners objected to this. They left Hertzog's party and founded a new one of their own – the Purified National Party. It was led by Dr Daniel Malan.

During the 1930s, the government took steps to keep white voters in control. In 1930, all white women over 21 were given the vote. In 1936, blacks lost the vote in the Cape. Instead, they were allowed to elect three white representatives under a separate system.

South African mines needed a lot of workers. However, if blacks were to work for whites, they had to live near enough to get to work. Mineworkers usually lived in compounds, close to the mines. Other black workers often lived in

shanty towns on the outskirts of cities. These grew fast during the Second World War. 'You might as well try to sweep the ocean back with a broom,' said the Prime Minister.

In 1945, the government decided that blacks who had lived and worked in white areas for a long time could become permanent residents. In 1948, it went a step further. It accepted a report which said that total **segregation** of blacks and whites was impossible: some blacks would have to live alongside whites.

The Purified National Party did not agree. Their aim had always been to keep black and white separate. They did not intend to stop now. The country was preparing itself for a General Election – and Dr Malan's supporters got ready to deal with the 'native problem' once and for all.

E *This is South Africa (1947).*

The Natives, often [for] their own protection, are treated by law in many respects as if they were children; they may not be supplied with European liquor; they must not be out after certain hours at night without a special pass; for them the curfew still rings in many of the country towns.

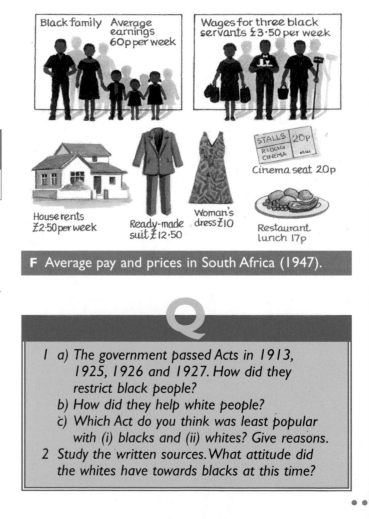

F Average pay and prices in South Africa (1947).

Q

1 a) The government passed Acts in 1913, 1925, 1926 and 1927. How did they restrict black people?
   b) How did they help white people?
   c) Which Act do you think was least popular with (i) blacks and (ii) whites? Give reasons.
2 Study the written sources. What attitude did the whites have towards blacks at this time?

A Word about Race

Four main racial groups lived in South Africa. These were the population figures for 1946:

- Black 7 805 515
- White 2 372 690
- Mixed 928 484
- Asiatics 285 260

Who was there first?

The earliest people in the area were the Khoi-san, who lived in the south. The first black settlers arrived from the north in about the 4th century AD. Within a century, they were living in parts of Transvaal and Natal. A thousand years later, they were living in the heart of modern South Africa.

White Dutch settlers first arrived in the 17th century. There were few Dutch women among them so the Dutch Commander encouraged mixed marriages from 1656 onwards and mixed-race children were born. There was little colour prejudice at this time. Whites often married black slaves, provided they had become Christians. However, in 1685, marriages between whites and blacks were banned.

A A Boer and his slave return after a day's hunting. This picture dates from 1804–5.

The Asiatics came last. Asian slaves were brought in during the late 17th century. The biggest group were Indians who arrived from 1860 onwards, to work on the sugar plantations.

Why does it matter?

It matters because Afrikaners claimed that the land really belonged to them because white people got there first. Until the 1990s, schoolchildren were taught that the land was almost empty when the whites arrived. Like much of Afrikaner **propaganda,** this was a lie.

Afrikaners despised the Khoi-san, who were certainly there first. One white person said 'the Bushman was a freak survival from some primitive age'. The word 'Hottentot' was a Dutch nickname, meaning 'stutterer', because their language included repeated clicking sounds.

Problems with language

The Afrikaners used their language as propaganda. For instance, the Afrikaans word Afrikaner means African – a white South African, who spoke Afrikaans. When an Afrikaner talked of South Africa, he meant white South Africa.

In 1900, local inhabitants in the British Empire were usually called natives. Most people stopped using the word after the Second World War but in South Africa it was still used in the 1990s. However, 'native' suggested that black people arrived in South Africa first. Afrikaners were keen to prove they did not.

So, during the 1960s, whites described the blacks as Bantu. The word, in many black African languages, simply means people. After the 1970s, they were known as 'blacks'.

However, in daily life, most whites used terms of abuse when they talked to blacks. They usually called blacks 'kaffir', meaning 'pagan'. It described someone you looked down upon. An adult black man was called 'boy' and adult black women were 'girls'. Blacks were expected to call white people 'baas', meaning 'boss'.

Blacks themselves generally called themselves 'Africans'. However, this did not always mean 'South African'; it meant someone who lived in black Africa – a continent which stretched from the Sahara Desert in the north to South Africa in the south.

Coloureds

Most mixed-race people lived in Cape Province and were the result of black-white marriages. During the 1930s, they were generally treated as if they were white. After the war, Afrikaners saw them as a separate group and called them Coloureds. Many did not like this name and preferred to call themselves 'Bastards'.

But the only way anyone could spot a 'Coloured' was by the colour of their skin. Some of them were so light that the person could live as a white person and no one would know they were Coloured. People called them 'play-whites'. One writer reckoned in 1935 that over 500 000 whites were really mixed-race. That was one in four of the white population.

The Zulu name for Johannesburg is EGoli. It means 'city of gold'. Whites usually called it Jo'burg.

Asiatics

This word was usually used to describe people who came from the Indian sub-continent. It was not applied to people from the Far East (e.g. Japanese) nor people from the Near East (e.g. Arabs). 'Asiatics' disliked the word and preferred to be called Asians.

Whites

To add to the confusion, whites were called blankes, meaning 'white' in Afrikaans. English-speakers usually translated this as 'Europeans', which annoyed Afrikaners. Afrikaners often thought of the whites as forming separate nations, although they were treated as one by the law. When blacks wrote about whites, they often used the word 'whiteman', as one word.

This book

In white South Africa, only Afrikaners really liked what they were called. So deciding how to describe people is a headache. Some books refer to blacks as 'Africans' but this may be misleading, for reasons given above.

The words most commonly used in this book are 'black', 'white' and 'Coloured'. However, in the next few chapters, the words 'native' and 'Bantu' crop up in laws passed by the government. You should remember that all these words were chosen by the Afrikaner minority and were unpopular with almost everyone else.

B Beauty treatments to turn skin lighter sold well in South Africa (1982).

C One Coloured said this to Anthony Samson (from *Drum*, 1956):

You white men, you're not our friends. We Coloured people – we didn't ask you to sleep with our black mothers. We didn't ask you to make bastards of us. And then you run away when our black mothers have children. You're our own cousins, man. And you don't even let us into your *bioscopes*. You cowards! You come and make friends with us, and then take our girls – and we can't take yours.

Q

1 a) Make notes about the different racial groups in South Africa. Write down who they were and how the Afrikaners described them
   b) What annoyed each group?
2 If you were writing a book about South African history, what would you call each group? Explain how you decided.

Just before the 1948 election, Dr Malan's National Party published the *Sauer Report*. This had studied the situation in South Africa and offered Afrikaners a stark choice.

> **A** The *Sauer Report*, 1948.
>
> The choice before us is one of these two courses: either *integration*, which would in the long run amount to national suicide on the part of the Whites; or 'apartheid', which [claims] to preserve the identity and safeguard the future of every race.

Two changes worried many Afrikaners. Firstly, blacks had started taking over skilled and semi-skilled jobs, although some whites were out of work; secondly, black workers were flocking to the towns and staying there. The National Party wanted to halt both these trends.

So voters were asked to choose. The United Party offered more integration; the National Party offered the policy of 'apartheid'. It was not clear exactly what apartheid meant but it definitely did not mean integration and it did not mean rights for blacks.

The National Party won the General Election. The Nationalists ruled South Africa until 1994.

C Dr Daniel Malan.

Dr Malan was 74 when he became Prime Minister. He had once been a preacher in the Dutch Reformed Church. He was a hard-line Afrikaner who wanted to keep the Afrikaner race pure. In other words, he wanted to keep them separate from everyone else. He was convinced that the Afrikaner people had been chosen by God to rule South Africa.

One day, when he was a young man, he saw some white children playing with Coloured ones. The sight affected him deeply. Long afterwards, he said this event gave him the idea of apartheid.

B South African policemen with batons disperse black rioters in Durban, 1949.

'Apartheid' is an Afrikaans word, meaning 'separateness'. So how was the new policy different to the segregation which already existed? At first, there was really no great difference. Even Dr Malan said the aims were the same.

In 1948, apartheid was a vague policy. The details were worked out, piece by piece, over a number of years. Many of the government's new laws were based on ones which already existed in 1948. In fact, many of the basic ideas were first introduced by the British in the 19th century.

The word 'apartheid' came to mean not only segregation but also white **domination** of all other races. The Afrikaners believed in baaskap (mastership). Over the next 15 years, Afrikaner governments kept making new laws to keep whites in charge. It is easiest to understand apartheid by first studying some of the main laws.

Population Registration Act (1950)

Before apartheid could be put into practice, the government needed to know who belonged to each racial group – white, native and Coloured. So a racial register was started after 1951. This register also divided natives and Coloureds into smaller groups. Whites were simply white.

Because of mixed marriages, this was easier said than done, as you saw on pages 6–7. Many whites had some black physical characteristics; some Coloureds looked white. So two criteria were used to decide which group a person belonged to: (1) actual colour and (2) the verdict of society.

In other words, if a person looked white but had usually been treated as a Coloured, then he or she was classified as Coloured. This led to the strange situation that some Afrikaner MPs looked Coloured but were classed as white, because that's how they were treated before 1950. It also caused some families to be split up.

This law was almost impossible to enforce. In the last resort, a court had to decide. But, 13 years later, there were still 20 000 individuals who had not been classified.

> **D** Anthony Sampson described the government's problem in *Drum* (1956).
>
> They were determined to find out who was, and who was not, white, coloured and native. Officials passed combs through the hair of Coloured men, and felt the lobes of their ears, in an attempt to prove that they were natives. In one case a man was classified as white, his brother as Coloured. Hundreds of whites were demoted to Coloureds, and Coloureds to natives: children with a trace of coloured blood were expelled from white schools.

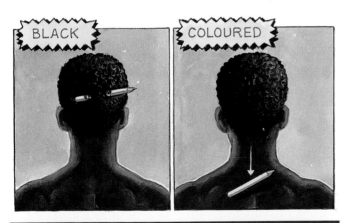

> **E** Which race? This was one crude test which officials used to find out. Another way was to look behind the ears.

Prohibition of Mixed Marriages Act (1949)

The second strand of apartheid was to make sure that the white race stayed white. This law banned marriages between whites and non-whites.

Immorality Amendment Act (1950)

This Act banned sex between whites and non-whites. The maximum punishment for those found guilty was six months' hard labour. (In 1957, this was increased to seven years.) Finding proof was difficult so police shone torches inside parked cars late at night and entered people's homes without warning.

Both whites and non-whites disliked this law. In any case, it did not stop 'illegal' sex. Over the next ten years, 3890 people were found guilty; convictions rose steadily. Sex between black and white went on unseen.

> **F** Anthony Sampson quoted a white man called Butch in *Drum* (1956).
>
> You think black men don't dance with white girls in Jo'burg, don't you? You know nothing, man. I could take you to places which make you gasp, man – right in the middle of your white Jo'burg. I was a cop. I know things. I know what cops do. Huh. Apartheid. You know what? Black likes white and white likes black.

> **G** Graham de Proft and Sonya. He threw himself under a train when she became pregnant in 1974. As a Coloured, he could not marry a white woman.

Q

1 a) What were the aims of apartheid?
   b) List the main details of the three laws on this page.
   c) How did each help to introduce apartheid?
2 Which law do you think was most unpopular with (a) blacks, (b) Coloureds and (c) whites? Explain how you decided.
3 What evidence is there that it was difficult to enforce these laws?

MORE APARTHEID LAWS

Group Areas Act (1950)

The government wanted to make sure that whites, blacks and Coloureds lived separately. The Group Areas Act divided South Africa into separate areas for the different races. Only one race would be allowed to live in each area and non-whites would be kept out of towns and cities. People who lived in the 'wrong' area would be forced to move. Of course, most of the country was reserved for whites so the people who suffered most were non-whites.

A	People who would be affected in Durban (1958):	
Indian 75 000		White 1000
Coloured 8500		

The Group Areas system never fully happened. The task was just too big. In 1980, over 60 per cent of blacks still lived outside 'their' areas. But it caused much misery and suffering: some people killed themselves when they learned they were going to be moved.

The government followed this up with a 1951 law which banned illegal **squatting.** This stopped anyone from entering any land or building without permission. Any buildings which the squatters put up were torn down.

B In 1949, the government stopped free milk being given to black children. There was a bad drought at the time and cattle were starving. In some black reserves, people were eating weeds to survive.

C A reference book, often called a pass book.

Pass laws

The Group Areas Act stated that people could only live in their own racial area. But there was a problem: you could not judge a person's race just by looking at their skin colour. So people needed to carry something to prove who they were and where they lived. And this is where the pass laws came in.

Pass laws existed before the Second World War for every black male over 16. Any black man without a pass or in the wrong area was put in prison and lost his job. Blacks found the pass system humiliating; even many whites complained about it. In 1952, the government decided to change the law – but not in the way blacks wanted.

Natives (Abolition of Passes and Coordination of Documents) Act (1952)

This Act did not do what its title said. Instead of *abolishing* passes, it actually *extended* them. From 1952 onwards, all blacks had to carry a reference book once they reached the age of 16. After 1956, black women also had to carry them. They needed separate passes to be out at night after nine pm.

The reference book contained 96 pages, with all sorts of information. However, the key contents were the owner's photograph, details of where they lived, any job they had and their fingerprint. In effect, the reference book was a pass. Blacks nicknamed it 'the stinker'. Other races were given an identity card but owners did not have to carry them round. If requested, they had seven days in which to present it. Non-whites were arrested if they did not have theirs. In a typical year, 400 000 people might be arrested.

Native Laws Amendment Act (1952)

The government followed this up with a law restricting black movement in white areas. This 1952 Act banned blacks from staying in urban areas for longer than 72 hours without a permit. There were exceptions for someone who had been born there or was a permanent resident.

Petty apartheid

The laws described so far formed the basis of apartheid. However, the government later produced one law after another to control even minor aspects of everyday life. Put together, these laws added up to what people called 'petty apartheid'.

For instance, in 1953, owners of public premises or vehicles could reserve them for use by just one race only, if they wished. They did not have to provide the same service for other races.

In 1955, the Motor Transport Act allowed organisations to introduce apartheid on public transport. Oddly, this meant the Johannesburg buses made a loss. An official said that they could make £500 000 profit a year if apartheid were stopped.

The year 1957 saw a new idea: a government minister was given the right to stop blacks attending church services in a white area. The Churches were so angry that the government did not enforce it. But that same year, apartheid was introduced into nursing and, in 1960, it was extended to beaches.

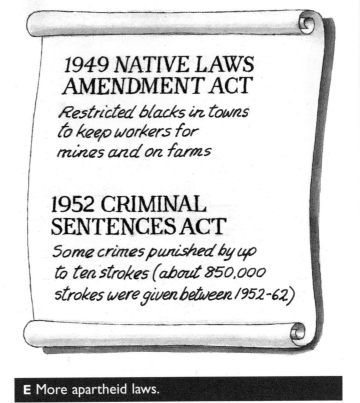

1949 NATIVE LAWS AMENDMENT ACT
Restricted blacks in towns to keep workers for mines and on farms

1952 CRIMINAL SENTENCES ACT
Some crimes punished by up to ten strokes (about 850,000 strokes were given between 1952-62)

E More apartheid laws.

White voters only

The Afrikaners were determined that only whites would control the government. In 1948, they stopped Indians being represented in parliament. But what really upset the Afrikaners was the fact that Coloureds had the vote. What upset them even more was that these voters nearly always voted against the Nationalists.

There were only about 48 000 Coloured voters but the Afrikaners were determined to get rid of them. They succeeded in 1956, after a long struggle. All Coloureds were taken off the common voting roll. Instead, they voted in a separate election; four white MPs represented them in parliament. The Afrikaners had finally got what they wanted back in 1910: a government chosen solely by white people.

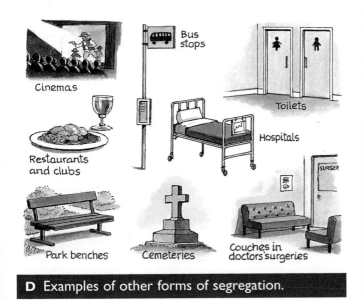

Cinemas

Restaurants and clubs

Park benches

Bus stops

Toilets

Hospitals

Cemeteries

Couches in doctors' surgeries

D Examples of other forms of segregation.

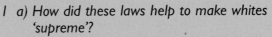

Q

1 a) How did these laws help to make whites 'supreme'?
   b) In what ways were non-whites treated as second-class citizens?
2 a) What impression do you now get of government attitudes towards non-whites?
   b) What do you think non-whites would feel about the government's attitude?

APARTHEID (1953–5)

Bantu Education Act (1953)

The mastermind behind the government's apartheid policy was Dr Verwoerd. He was Minister of Native Affairs from 1950 to 1958, when he became Prime Minister. Verwoerd was convinced that his power came directly from God. He once told a reporter, 'I do not have the nagging doubt of ever wondering whether I am wrong'.

Verwoerd was probably the cleverest Afrikaner politician. He knew apartheid was unpopular abroad. As Prime Minister, he tried to make it seem a positive policy which benefited black people.

In 1953, Dr Verwoerd's Native Affairs Department took over black schools. He decided that black children would be taught in their tribal language. They would follow a different syllabus to white pupils. Black pupils, he argued, did not need to learn what white children did. But they would learn that they were not equal to whites.

A Some of Dr Verwoerd's ideas about black education. (At this point, Afrikaners were beginning to talk of 'Bantus', rather than 'natives'.)

Teaching the Bantu in English or Afrikaans would only make Bantus think they had a place among the civilised in South Africa.

The school must equip [a black pupil] to meet the demands which South Africa will impose upon him. There is no place for the native in the European community above the level of certain forms of labour.

What is the use of teaching a Bantu child mathematics when it cannot use it in practice? That is absurd.

At the same time, he announced that black teachers needed less pay than white ones. After 1963, black teachers earned a maximum of £320 a year; the minimum salary for a white male teacher was £603. There were other cuts, too. Black schools were given less equipment and no money to repair buildings or replace furniture. Black pupils' parents had to buy their own writing materials.

In 1959, the government went a step further and started to ban non-white students from mixed universities. Instead, it set up new colleges along racial lines for non-whites. White lecturers who opposed apartheid were sacked.

B Spending on school pupils before cuts were made (1953):

Whites £63.92
Coloured & Asians £20.21
Blacks £8.99

C Transvaal textbooks were written to include Nationalist propaganda. These are two extracts:

Although our *forefathers* had been in daily contact with the non-White inhabitants, there was [almost] no inter-marrying.

The White stands on a much higher plane of civilization and is more developed [than the non-White]. Whites must so live, learn and work that we shall not sink to the level of the non-Whites.

D Dr Verwoerd is shown in this cartoon from a South African newspaper (1990).

Sophiatown

In 1905, a small township had grown up just four miles from the centre of Johannesburg. It was called Sophiatown. It was in open country, right next to a sewage farm, where whites did not want to live. But Johannesburg grew and white people built their houses up to, and around, Sophiatown.

The township was special for two reasons. The inhabitants came from various races and many of them actually owned their homes. So Sophiatown was a challenge to the Nationalists: non-whites were living in a 'white area'. In 1954, the government passed the Natives Resettlement Act. The plan was to move all of the 57 000 people out of Sophiatown to a new area.

E Sophiatown before the evictions.

Their new homes would be further from Johannesburg, in a new township with the romantic name of Meadowlands. But they would not own these houses. The town would build them and rent them to tenants.

Much of Sophiatown had become a slum and Dr Verwoerd said that the inhabitants would be healthier living elsewhere. However, the township was better than many other areas where blacks lived. The only swimming pool for Johannesburg's black inhabitants was in Sophiatown.

The opposition was enormous. Even politicians of other parties were against the Nationalists' plan. But Dr Verwoerd organised a clever propaganda campaign. He said that opponents were trying to stop slum clearance: they were being unfair to the blacks.

In January 1955, the first 152 families were told they would leave in February. Extra police moved into the area, jeered by local people.

Slogans were painted everywhere: 'Hands off Sophiatown' and 'This is home'. There were rumours of plans to stop the eviction.

At 6.00 am on 9th February, 2000 police were in the area. Lorries drove up and people's possessions were piled on board. There was no resistance. There was nothing that the inhabitants could do.

When they had gone, demolition squads climbed on to the houses and demolished them with pick-axes and sledge-hammers. But it took six years to destroy Sophiatown completely. It was replaced by a white suburb, Triomf ('triumph').

G Nelson Mandela tried to organise resistance to the eviction. He described how the failure affected him in *Long Walk to Freedom* (1995).

The lesson I took away from the campaign was that, in the end, we had no alternative to armed and violent resistance. Over and over again, we had used all the non-violent weapons [but] whatever we did was met by an iron hand. A freedom fighter learns the hard way. At a certain point, one can only fight fire with fire.

F ...and afterwards.

Q

1 a) What was the government's aim in education?
   b) What do you think the effects were?
2 a) Why did the government want to destroy Sophiatown?
   b) Why did the inhabitants want to stay?
   c) Why was there very little resistance?
   d) What conclusion did Mandela draw from this?

The African National Congress

In 1910, the Union of South Africa deprived most blacks of any say in their future. In 1912, the African National Congress (ANC) was founded to cut across tribal divisions by uniting all black Africans. Separate organisations were set up to represent Indians and Coloureds.

The ANC's founders wanted to protect black people's rights by peaceful actions. Its leaders were educated middle-class blacks, such as lawyers and ministers. However, by 1939, it had achieved very little. In fact, restrictions on blacks had increased.

In 1943, a Youth League was started, led by a young lawyer called Anton Lembede. Two years later, the ANC stated that their aims were to end the colour bar and get black people the vote. But when Dr Malan's National Party came to power in 1948, it was clear that conditions for blacks would grow worse.

In 1949, a major split developed between the older members and the Youth League. Younger members wanted the ANC to take more **militant** action to achieve equality. Walter Sisulu became the ANC's secretary-general and the ANC adopted a new Programme of Action. This would involve strikes, demonstrations and other forms of **civil disobedience.** The ANC had set out on a course which it was to follow for over 40 years.

Suppression of Communism Act (1950)

The ANC organised a 'Freedom Day' on May 1 1950, when workers went on strike. The government did not want this to happen again so, in June, it passed the Suppression of Communism Act.

Under this law, almost any opposition to the government was treated as communism – and therefore banned. For instance, anyone using using 'disturbance or disorder' to change politics, industry or society in South Africa counted as a communist.

Anyone found guilty could be sent to jail for up to ten years. However, prosecutions were rare. The law's main purpose was to give the government a huge range of powers against its opponents. It could ban communists or ex-communists from sitting in Parliament. It could ban any communist publication. It could ban anyone at all from attending a public meeting.

This law made almost any opposition to the government illegal. In effect, it became illegal to oppose either apartheid or white supremacy. And this was what the government wanted.

B What happened to a banned person (1954 onwards). Over 1500 people were banned at some stage by the Nationalists.

Defiance campaign (1952)

The ANC and the Indian Congress reacted by holding a '**defiance** campaign' against six laws they thought were unjust, including the one described above.

A This peaceful demonstration on June 26 1952 was part of the defiance campaign.

By the end of the year, 8065 volunteers had deliberately broken various apartheid laws. They included a few whites. Each went to jail for one to three weeks. The campaign ended in 1953 but it had one major effect: ANC membership shot up from 7000 to 100 000.

The government replied with the Criminal Law Amendment Act (1953). This made it illegal to break any other law as a protest. The maximum punishment was a £300 fine, three years in prison and ten lashes. Anyone who encouraged someone else to protest faced an even stiffer punishment. Passive resistance, was also illegal now.

Freedom Charter (1955)

The ANC organised other campaigns – against Bantu education and, in 1956, against the Pass Laws. But it was still a mainly peaceful movement. In 1952, Chief Albert Luthuli became its new leader.

He encouraged the ANC to form links with other organisations which wanted change in South Africa. In 1955, they held a Congress of the People at Kliptown, near Johannesburg. There were representatives from:

- African National Congress
- South Africa Indian Congress
- Coloured People's Congress
- Congress of Democrats (whites)

E Police try to intimidate workers walking to town during the 1956 bus boycott.

This Congress Alliance drew up a list of basic demands. They were so basic that they already existed in every true **democracy** in the world. The government decided that the Freedom Charter was an act of treason and charged 156 people under the Suppression of Communism Act. The trial lasted from 1956 to 1961 and became known as the 'Treason Trial'. All of the defendants were found not guilty.

Pan-Africanist Congress (PAC)

In 1959, some ex-ANC members set up a new organisation – the Pan Africanist Congress of Azania (PAC). They did not support the Freedom Charter and believed that blacks should work alone to achieve their rights. Its first leader was Robert Sobukwe.

Q

1 a) What were the ANC's aims?
   b) Why did it change its methods after the war?
   c) How successful were its protests?
2 Study the Freedom Charter (Source D). Choose any five points and explain what the situation in South Africa actually was. Use the earlier pages to provide information.
3 You are an ANC leader in 1959. What would you do next to achieve your aims? Explain how you decided.

Massacre at Sharpeville (1960)

In February 1960, British Prime Minister Harold Macmillan ended a tour of Africa. At Cape Town, he made a speech to the South African parliament. He told MPs that the British government did not approve of apartheid and warned them that they could not ignore black demands.

A This part of his speech became famous:

The most striking impression I have formed is of the strength of African national consciousness. The wind of change is blowing through this continent, and whether we like it or not, this growth of national consciousness is a political fact.

The Nationalists did not like it. Nor did they agree that change had to come. Dr Verwoerd told Macmillan that apartheid did meet the needs of black Africans.

Black people, of course, did not agree. They had many complaints against the apartheid system. For instance, protests against the Pass Laws were quite common. In 1956, 20 000 women had marched to the government buildings in Pretoria to complain. The usual punishment for not having your pass book was a month in prison or a £10 fine.

The ANC decided to protest against the Pass Laws on 31 March 1960. But the PAC decided to act first. It announced a mass campaign, to start ten days before the ANC's action.

The PAC's wanted all blacks to leave their pass books at home and go to their local police station to admit they were breaking the law. The theory was that the police could not lock up every black person: the prisons were just not big enough.

The PAC did not intend any violence. It planned a peaceful protest, starting on March 21, in various towns. One of them was the black township of Sharpeville, 35 miles from Johannesburg. It was generally known as a quiet place. Even the government thought that Sharpeville was a model township.

There are two versions of almost everything that happened that day. At dawn, local leaders went from door-to-door, handing out leaflets and asking people not to go to work. Pickets were set up near the bus station to stop people boarding buses.

Some people claimed this was not done peacefully. They said that people kicked doors down and forced those inside to join the protest. Certainly, the demonstration grew larger and eventually a procession set off for the police station. It arrived at about 8.00 am.

It was a large and excited crowd, however big it was. Some sources claimed it was happy and peaceful and that no one carried any weapons. The police claimed that it was aggressive and that some people did have weapons, including stones, which were thrown at the police.

At 10.00 am, aircraft flew backwards and forwards over the crowd, as though they were trying to scare people away. Later that morning, a rumour went round that a top official would be coming to address the crowd. At 1.15 pm, Lieutenant-Colonel Pienaar, a senior police officer, turned up.

He was accompanied by a Saracen armoured car and police with automatic weapons. Shortly afterwards, Pienaar lined up 75 white policemen outside the station and ordered them each to load five rounds.

Quite what happened next has never been made clear. No one heard warning shots. Some people claimed there was an order to open fire; others said there wasn't. But that is what the police did. The shooting lasted 10–30 seconds. When it began, the demonstrators quickly turned and fled.

B People running from bullets after the shooting started at Sharpeville.

F The mass burial of the Sharpeville victims at the end of March, 1960

What, exactly, happened?

C *Chronicle of the 20th Century* (1988).

In one of the worst civilian massacres in South African history, 56 Africans died and 162 were injured when police opened fire in the black township of Sharpeville in the Transvaal. In other disturbances, seven died and 209 were injured at the Langa township near Cape Town.

D Douglas Brown: *Against the World* (1966).

... Sharpeville, the massacre in which 67 Africans were killed and 186 wounded, most of them having been shot in the back.

E Modiehi Mahabane was a Sharpeville resident. In 1990, she recalled:

I was standing at the door, quite nervous, when two white policemen called me. They asked me to give them water. I took a jug and took the water to them... They said, 'You know, at two o'clock, we are going to start shooting.'

G Encyclopaedia Britannica Yearbook for 1960 (1961).

The official total was 67 Africans dead and 186 wounded, 48 women and children being among the victims. At the Langa township in Cape Town, on the same day, large anti-pass demonstrations resulted in the death of one African, the wounding of many others and the destruction of much property.

H *The Times* (British newspaper), March 22 1960.

After shooting in the morning, in which one African was killed and another seriously wounded, a crowd of several hundred Africans this afternoon began stoning the police armoured cars. Quite suddenly, there were bursts of firing, chiefly from Sten guns. The mob scattered, leaving about 80 people sprawled on the ground in a growing pool of blood.

I Joanmarie Fubbs was a white reporter (1990).

I saw a policeman taking his rifle-butt to several women who were trying to retrieve bodies. They weren't shot down but they were rifle-butted and kicked and booted.

Q

1 List any facts which are not disputed.
2 a) Which sources do you think are most reliable and why?
*   b) Which sources do you think are least reliable and why?*
*   c) Write your own account of the event, based on the sources you trust.*
3 Why do you think it is still not possible to be certain about the number of dead and wounded?

AFTER SHARPEVILLE

A Protestors demonstrating after the Sharpeville massacre.

Heavy rain fell on Sharpeville early that afternoon. It washed away the blood from the road and the bodies. But the bloodshed had a more lasting effect on the Nationalist government and on South African history.

Photographs of dead bodies were printed in newspapers around the world. There was shock and outrage. The USA condemned it. In April, the UN Security Council asked South Africa to abandon apartheid. It condemned the shootings, although Britain and France **abstained.**

In the next few days, there were riots in South Africa; 86 more people were killed. About 30 000 people marched through Cape Town to protest. The Chief of Police promised the march's leader a meeting if he got the crowd to go home. He did but, when he returned for the meeting, he was arrested. A strike of black workers in the city lasted almost three weeks.

On March 28, the ANC organised a protest day, when people stayed away from work. It was followed by a mass burning of passes. Chief Luthuli and Nelson Mandela burnt theirs.

B But world criticism made many Afrikaners more determined than ever. Dr Verwoerd said:

> The white man of Africa is not going to be told that, because he is outnumbered by the black people, he must allow his rights to be swallowed up.

The government claimed that Sharpeville had all been a communist plot. On March 30, it declared a State of Emergency, which lasted until August. This gave the government almost total powers to deal with anybody for any reason. One week later, both the ANC and Pan-African Congress were banned.

About 20 000 opponents of apartheid were rounded up, including Mandela. Robert Sobukwe was sent to prison for three years. Some people were held without trial; others were tried secretly inside the jails. Thousands were sent to a work camp or prison, where many died because of over-crowding. A year later, the government passed the General Law Amendment Act. It allowed them to detain anybody for up to 12 days, without bail.

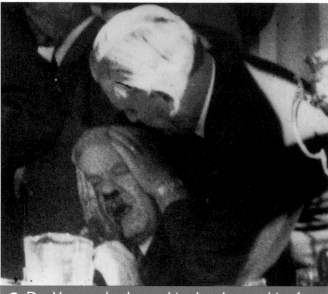

C Dr Verwood clasps his hands to his face immediately after having been shot.

In April 1960, Dr Verwoerd was shot in the head by a white farmer (source C). Many people thought he would die and hoped this would lead to a change in government policies. But Verwoerd did not die. Within two months, he was back at work. His supporters believed that his recovery was the work of God.

Nor did he change his policies. He was hurt that the world did not understand apartheid. Nationalists pointed out that black people's earnings were three times what they had earned back in 1910. Dr Verwoerd claimed that apartheid was in black people's own interests; even the State of Emergency was for their own good.

> Many white South Africans never shook hands with blacks. Some believed that the black colour could be transferred by sweat.

D Members of the Black Sash organisation demonstrated outside Johannesburg's city hall (1961). They were opposed to apartheid.

South Africa leaves the Commonwealth

Before the Sharpeville massacre, Verwoerd decided to hold a **referendum** to decide whether South Africa should become a republic. Only whites were allowed to vote and, in October, they chose to become a republic.

Dr Verwoerd attended the Commonwealth Conference in March 1961, wanting South Africa to remain a member. However, apartheid was unpopular with other countries and they pressed him to change his policy. Instead, he decided that South Africa should leave the Commonwealth. Two months later, on May 31 1961, South Africa officially became a republic.

Before the First World War, some Boer leaders had wanted to be free to run their country without interference from Britain. Just 51 years after the Union of South Africa was created, that dream had come true. The government no longer had to worry about what Britain wanted: it could do as it wished, even if the entire world disapproved. Which it did.

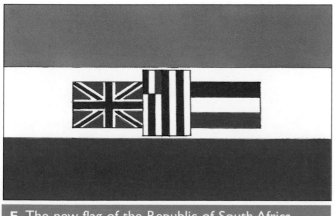

E The new flag of the Republic of South Africa.

Economic consequences

The events of 1960 damaged the country's economy for a while. About £100 million was withdrawn by foreign investors. Some people refused to buy South African goods. The world was not just opposed to apartheid; it was worried about future conflicts and how they might harm business.

However, none of this did much harm to Dr Verwoerd's National Party. They easily won the General Election in 1961. Their total of MPs was almost double that of all other parties put together. They still had the power to pass whatever laws they wished – and Dr Verwoerd was determined to do so.

Footnote

A Court of Enquiry was later held to look into events at Sharpeville. The judge concluded that the shootings were 'deliberate and unnecessary'. Yet no one was ever put on trial for the killings. Families of those killed never received compensation. The government passed a law which said it could not be taken to court over the massacre.

F Afrikaners celebrating the fifth anniversary of South Africa becoming a republic (1966).

Q

1 a) What were the consequences of the Sharpeville massacre (i) abroad and (ii) inside South Africa?
 b) Which one do you think most worried the South African government?
2 At this point, what could be done to change apartheid:
 a) by South African blacks;
 b) by South African whites;
 c) by other countries?
3 Look at your answers to question 2. Do you think any of these ideas would work? Explain your answer.

One person arrested after Sharpeville was a young black lawyer who would play a major role in South Africa's history. His name was Nelson Mandela.

He was born in 1918, a member of the royal family of the Tembu people. His father died when he was young and the chief brought him up. When Mandela found that the chief had arranged a marriage for him, he ran away to Johannesburg where he studied law at the University of Witwatersrand.

In 1947, he became the ANC Youth League's secretary and was chosen as 'Volunteer-in-Chief' for the Defiance Campaign in 1952. As a result, he was tried under the Suppression of Communism Act. Although found guilty, he was only given a suspended sentence. That same year, he set up the first black law firm in Johannesburg with another ANC supporter called Oliver Tambo.

In a dawn raid on December 5 1956, Mandela was one of the 156 people arrested and accused of high treason. Others were Chief Luthuli and Walter Sisulu. The trial did not end until 1961, after the Sharpeville massacre. All the defendants were found not guilty.

> Mandela's second name is Rolihlahla, which means 'stirring up trouble' in Xhosa.

Oliver Tambo was another of the defendants. During the trial, in 1960, he slipped out of the country and went into exile abroad. He set up offices elsewhere in Africa and in Europe. It was an important step for the ANC because it could now gain publicity abroad to support its cause. Tambo remained in exile until 1990.

B Nelson Mandela, speaking in the Treason Trial.

We are not anti-white. We are against white supremacy. In struggling against white supremacy, we have the support of some sections of the European population. The ANC has consistently preached a policy of race harmony and we have condemned racialism by [anybody].

A Tambo (left) and Mandela in the 1950s.

When Mandela became President of the Transvaal section of the ANC, the government banned him from attending public meetings and stopped him from leaving Johannesburg. In 1953, a new two-year banning order stopped him from attending the Congress which drew up the Freedom Charter. However, he supported it totally. When the second banning order ran out, the government banned him for another five years. Despite this, he went on working secretly for the ANC.

C The defendants in the Treason Trial. Mandela is standing in the centre of the second row (1956).

'Umkhonto we Sizwe' (MK)

After Sharpeville, the ANC and PAC were both banned. Each turned its thoughts to armed struggle and set up military wings to organise violent opposition. The ANC's was called 'Umkhonto we Sizwe' (meaning 'Spear of the Nation'). It was commonly known as MK.

The ANC became an underground organisation. Mandela worked for it secretly, with the police always looking for him. He used various disguises. People nicknamed him 'the Black Pimpernel' because he seemed so elusive.

MK set up its HQ at a building in Rivonia, one of Johannesburg's fashionable suburbs. It bombed targets such as pass offices, post offices and electricity pylons. The first ten explosions happened in December 1961.

D A bomb placed in a car destroyed these buildings.

Mandela slipped out of South Africa in early 1962, to visit other countries to gain support. He returned to South Africa in June and was soon arrested. Police had no proof that he was involved with Umkhonto we Sizwe. Instead, he was charged with minor offences – organising strikes and leaving South Africa without a valid passport.

He knew he would be found guilty. As he told the court, 'I am a black man in a white man's court'. He was, indeed, found guilty and sentenced to five years' hard labour. He was sent to Robben Island, an offshore prison near Cape Town.

Mandela might have become just another unknown prisoner, had it not been for the government. While he was in prison, an informer gave police details of the Rivonia HQ. In 1963 they arrested six whites and 12 non-whites in Rivonia.

The Rivonia Trial (1963)

During 1962, the government passed a new law, usually known as the **Sabotage** Act. In brief, anyone found guilty of sabotage could be sentenced to death. The defendants at the Rivonia Trial were accused of sabotage. They included Mandela, though the police could not even prove at his last trial that he had any links with Umkhonto we Sizwe.

The police produced evidence of a deliberate campaign of sabotage planned at the Rivonia HQ. White South Africans were horrified. Mandela admitted that he had helped to set up MK. He also admitted planning acts of sabotage. There was no doubt he would be found guilty. However, under South African law, a defendant can address the court before the sentence is passed. Mandela read out a statement which lasted for four and a half hours. It was a milestone in South African history. Mandela, along with some other defendants, was sentenced to life imprisonment. He was still under a banning order which meant that South African newspapers were not allowed to quote him.

E Douglas Brown explained why in *Against the World* (1966).

What he said made little impact on the Court, or on white South Africa. This was the stage in the proceedings at which white reporters tend to slip out of Court for a cup of coffee. I have heard several such speeches, that [tell] of the suffering of a people and makes the white man's Court seem suddenly irrelevant. Few of them have been locally reported. But Mandela's speech has echoed round the world and been translated into a dozen languages.

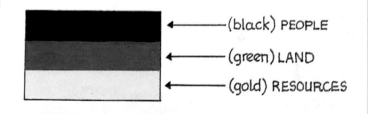

(black) PEOPLE
(green) LAND
(gold) RESOURCES

F The flag of the African National Congress and what it stood for. (It was chosen in 1925.)

Q

1 Draw a timeline to show Mandela's involvement in the ANC from 1947 to 1963. Allow 1cm for each year.
2 a) How did the Rivonia Trial help the government?
  b) How did it help the ANC?
  c) Who benefited most? Give reasons.
3 Blacks saw Mandela as a martyr. Would it have been better, for the government, if he had been sentenced to death? Give reasons.

The government said its policy was 'separate but equal development' for each race in South Africa. But Nationalists did not think of black people as one race, but as many. That way, blacks were not in the majority, after all.

> **A** *Progress Through Separate Development* was an official government publication (1973).
>
> **South Africa is a country of many nations: Four million whites of European origin, four million Xhosa, four million Zulu, two million Tswana, two million Sotho and so on. Each group is a minority – there is in fact no single majority group.**

In 1951, the government decided that all blacks should live in their own 'Bantustans' (homelands). They were based in the old reserves, first set up in 1913. The whites claimed that these were the traditional homes of blacks. In fact, this was untrue.

Only 13.7 per cent of South Africa was set aside for these bantustans but the amount provided was even less. Most farmland was of poor quality and there were very few jobs inside the bantustans. Some of the bantustans were very overcrowded. The inhabitants generally lived in very poor conditions indeed.

The government appointed a **commission** to recommend how to make the system work. Its report in 1954 said that the bantustans would need industry to provide jobs. This would cost £104 millions over ten years. Even then, more reserves would be needed to accommodate all black people. Also, the separate areas needed to be linked up.

The government largely ignored the report.

The Promotion of Bantu Self-Government Act (1959)

This set up eight bantustans. (Later, there were ten.) Each would have its own government, which could take a limited range of decisions but the South African government could **veto** any law it did not like. In return for their limited rights in the bantustans, black people would lose their rights elsewhere in South Africa.

In 1959, a Bantu Investment Corporation, run by whites, was set up to develop the economies of the bantustans. It had just £500 000 to do the job. Most of it was spent setting up shops and cafés, which could not possibly provide enough jobs for everyone.

In effect, the bantustans were little different from the old reserves: they were sources of cheap labour for white people, especially for unskilled jobs on farms or in industries owned by whites.

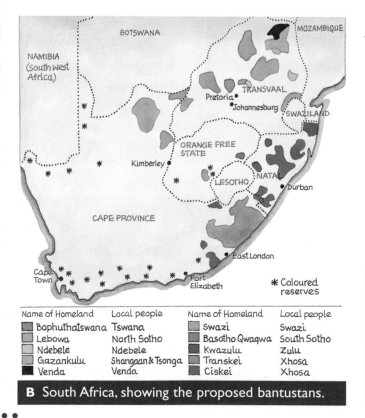

B South Africa, showing the proposed bantustans.

Name of Homeland	Local people	Name of Homeland	Local people
Bophuthatswana	Tswana	Swazi	Swazi
Lebowa	North Sotho	Basotho Qwaqwa	South Sotho
Ndebele	Ndebele	Kwazulu	Zulu
Gazankulu	Shangaan & Tsonga	Transkei	Xhosa
Venda	Venda	Ciskei	Xhosa

✳ Coloured reserves

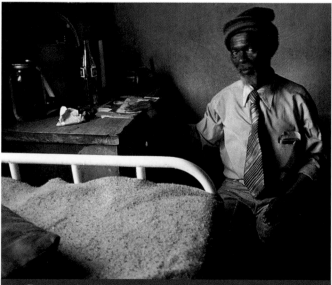

C Frederick Jillie lived in a hostel, 500 miles away from his wife and children. For 13 years, he saw them for only two and a half weeks each year, during his holiday (1972).

The bantustans gave the government a legal reason to get rid of black people whom they did not want in white areas. Old people, wives and children who were not needed in industry could be forced to live on the bantustan. The system kept the white economy working – and got rid of the blacks whom whites did not need.

In practice, this meant that a black person who found a job in a white area had three choices, depending on where his job was:

- become a **migrant** worker, living in a hostel, apart from his family.
- commute daily. This involved long bus journeys. Workers in KwaNdebele spent up to eight hours every day travelling to Pretoria and back. Some buses left at 2.30 am.
- live in a squatter camp with his family. If they were discovered, they might all be sent back to the bantustan and he would lose his job.

D Conditions in a squatter camp.

The Transkei (1963)

In 1963, the Transkei became the first bantustan to have its own parliament, elected by blacks. It was the biggest reserve and all in one place. The Transkei was created mainly for people of the Xhosa tribe, whether they lived there or not.

The Transkei's chief minister did not always agree with the South African government. For instance, the Transkei allowed sexual relations between whites and non-whites, although Chief Matanzima later asked all whites to leave the bantustan.

In 1970, the government made every black a citizen of a bantustan, wherever he or she lived. Even so, by 1980, only 54 per cent of those who should have lived in the bantustans actually did so.

The government promised that eventually blacks would govern their own bantustans. Dr Verwoerd even said that they might one day become independent. In 1976, the Transkei was given 'independence' by the South African government; other 'independent' bantustans followed – Bophuthatswana (1978), Venda (1979) and Ciskei (1981).

The rest of the world did not recognise these new 'nations'. Chief Buthelezi, leader of the Zulus, rejected independence for KwaZulu because he opposed the government's policies.

F This photograph shows the Zamani Soweto Sisters 'self-help' group at work (1982). It wasn't only the bantustans who were becoming 'independent'; the government's approval of the bantustans encouraged many others as well.

Q

1 Which of these statements do you agree with? (Explain your decisions.)
a) Bantustans benefited blacks and whites;
b) The Transkei was never really independent;
c) There was no majority race in South Africa.

Between 1946 and 1980, the United Nations passed 158 **resolutions** concerning South Africa. Indeed, apartheid was discussed at the UN during its very first session in 1946. On many occasions, the UN condemned apartheid, as in 1960, after Sharpeville.

However, attempts to impose **sanctions** on South Africa were not very successful. It was an issue which split world leaders. Some countries wanted to introduce sanctions to stop trade with South Africa. Others thought this would just make the Afrikaners more determined to keep apartheid. Britain did not support any sanctions against South Africa until 1964, when the General Assembly banned arms sales to the country.

In any case, the UN knew that sanctions could not work completely. South Africa was the richest country in southern Africa and almost self-sufficient. The whole of southern Africa's economy depended on South Africa. Other African countries needed South African goods.

Elsewhere in the world, some countries wanted to trade with her. The USA, Britain and France all increased their trade with South Africa in the 1950s and 1960s. When the Security Council tried to insist on sanctions in 1970, Britain, France and the USA all vetoed the proposal. They thought South Africa was a useful partner against communism. (Oddly, the Soviet Union openly criticised South Africa but still sold arms to the government.)

In 1971, Britain provided about 70 per cent of all foreign investment in South Africa. Foreign firms wanted to invest there, partly because there was a large supply of low-paid workers.

Other African countries tried to take action against South Africa. In 1963, the Organization of African Unity (OAU) expelled South Africa and asked its members to close their air space to South African planes. But countries like Kenya which stopped trade only found that other countries stepped in to take their place.

Sporting links

Sanctions were more successful in sport. Afrikaners were very keen on sport, especially rugby and cricket. They did not want to be kept out of international sporting events. But all sports facilities in South Africa were segregated so other countries took action.

B Sporting actions against South Africa.

1959 West Indies cricket tour abandoned.
1964 South Africa banned from Olympic Games.
1969 Demonstrations against Springbok rugby tour of Britain.
1970 Cricket tour to England cancelled by the MCC.
1977 Gleneagles agreement: Commonwealth banned sporting contacts

These actions had only a limited effect. In 1976, mixed-race teams were allowed to represent South Africa at international level. But clubs inside South Africa mostly remained segregated. This playing field was for blacks only.

Industrial production

Mineral production

Motor vehicles

Railway freight

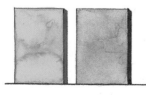

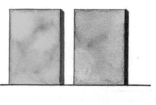

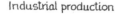

South Africa   Rest of Africa

A South Africa's wealth made her powerful (1973).

C Black children play football on a dusty field.

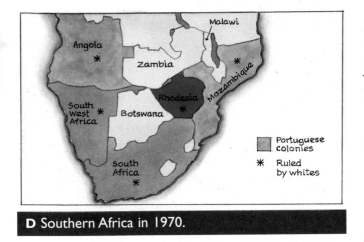

D Southern Africa in 1970.

Dr Verwoerd was keen to get on well with other African countries. What helped him was that most of the newly-independent African countries were poor and needed to trade with South Africa. In 1966, Verwoerd was **assassinated.** The new prime minister, John Vorster, continued a policy of **détente** with black African states.

He was helped because most of southern Africa was still ruled by whites. In 1965, the white minority government of Rhodesia had declared independence and left the British Commonwealth. There were strong links between the two countries.

Botswana only became independent in 1966 and could not afford to be aggressive: it was almost surrounded by South African troops. Also, it was a poor country; many inhabitants made their living in South Africa.

Malawi was the most friendly black nation towards white South Africa. But Dr Banda, its president, had little choice. Many of his people also worked as migrant labourers in South Africa and there were other close economic ties. He was the first black African leader to pay an official visit to South Africa; Mr Vorster visited Malawi in 1970.

Vorster's detente policy continued into the 1970s. Dr Kaunda, President of Zambia, held talks with Mr Vorster in 1975. UN sanctions against white Rhodesia had badly hurt his country's economy. He hoped that South Africa could help to end white minority rule in Rhodesia.

The talks came to nothing but they were a sign of how much black Africa needed South Africa's help. It seemed as though détente was working. But, just months later, the policy was ruined, partly because of events in South West Africa.

South West Africa (Namibia)

South West Africa had been a German colony until the First World War. In 1919, the League of Nations gave South Africa a **mandate** over the land to prepare it for independence. Instead, South Africa kept control over South-West Africa and introduced apartheid.

The UN protested; the International Court of Justice condemned South Africa; the South African government ignored them both, refusing to allow South West Africa independence.

South West Africa was even more racist than South Africa! Most of the white settlers were German; during the 1930s, children had worn swastika armbands and chanted 'Kill the Jews'.

Much of the population supported Hitler during the Second World War. Smuts rounded up Nazi leaders in 1939 and Mr Vorster himself was jailed for supporting a fascist organisation. Later, South West African whites were amongst Vorster's strongest supporters.

E Mr Vorster later said:

> If I had to live my life again, I would do exactly the same. I'm quite satisfied what I did was right.

The country's blacks outnumbered whites by seven to one. But the whites were in control; this provided South Africa with a buffer against black opponents in the north. But, in 1966, guerrillas of the South West African People's Organisation (SWAPO) began fighting the South African army. In 1971, the UN recognised SWAPO as the true representatives of Namibia. (This was what the rest of the world called South West Africa.)

The situation in southern Africa changed in the 1970s. In 1974, there was a revolution in Portugal and in 1975, Mozambique and Angola became independent. However, there was a civil war in Angola between UNITA, backed by western Europe and MPLA, backed by the Soviet Union and Cuba.

South Africa sent troops to help UNITA, an action which was condemned in the United Nations. It was also condemned in black Africa, which supported the MPLA. Most African countries were now united against South Africa.

Q

1 a) Why didn't sanctions against South Africa work? (There's more than one reason.)
   b) Why do you think British firms continued to trade with South Africa, despite apartheid?
2 a) What were South Africa's relations with neighbouring countries? Explain each one in turn.
   b) Why was South Africa's situation in 1976 more difficult than in 1970?

Soweto (1976)

In the early 1970s, opposition to apartheid grew inside South Africa. Trade unions took more militant action against anti-strike laws. During 1975, it became clear that black movements were preparing to increase the armed struggle.

There was most resistance in Soweto, a black township about ten miles outside Johannesburg. Many people from Sophiatown were sent here when it was destroyed. It was the biggest township, with an official population of 800 000. The real figure may have been more like 1.3 million. Over 200 000 of them commuted daily by train to work in Johannesburg. (The average journey took over four hours, there and back.)

Soweto was so overcrowded that many families shared houses. A four-room house might have a dozen or more people living in it. Most houses did not have electricity, indoor toilets or an indoor water supply. Outdoor taps supplied cold water only. Heat came from coal fires; lighting was by candles, and paraffin or gas lamps.

Thousands of migrant workers lived in single-sex hostels. One room housed up to eight people; there was no heating; visitors of the opposite sex (even wives and children) were banned. Some streets did not even have houses: people lived in shacks made from packing cases, cardboard boxes and bits of cars.

A Part of Soweto in 1976. Residents nicknamed these buildings 'matchbox houses'.

'Soweto' stood for SOuth-WEstern TOwnships. It was really a jumble of separate townships, covering about 34 square miles. Soweto had few facilities – a cinema, a few dance halls and beer-halls which were owned by the government. There was just one hospital. Even this was better than in most townships.

Alcoholism was common; so was violence. At least 12 people were murdered in a typical week-end; 40 died during the Christmas holiday. Soweto had the highest murder rate in the world.

What was unusual about Soweto was the high proportion of young people. In 1976, over half of them were under 20 years of age. They were generally more militant about apartheid than their parents.

In 1976, the government decided that some lessons would be taught in Afrikaans in black schools. This was rather like British pupils being taught in German during the war. For young blacks, Afrikaans was the symbol of oppression: it was the language of white supremacy. However, students had other reasons to complain, as source B shows.

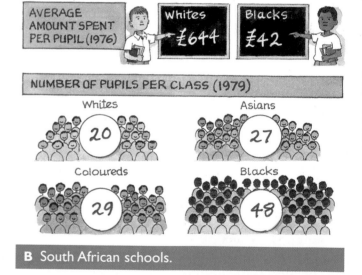

AVERAGE AMOUNT SPENT PER PUPIL (1976) — Whites £644 — Blacks £42

NUMBER OF PUPILS PER CLASS (1979)

Whites 20 Asians 27 Coloureds 29 Blacks 48

B South African schools.

Secondary school pupils **boycotted** examinations as a protest. Trouble began on June 16 when 20 000 schoolchildren staged a march. The police arrived to stop the march and the children mocked them.

Eye-witnesses disagreed about what happened next. Some said that children threw stones, then the police opened fire; others said that the stones were only thrown after the police fired tear gas. Certainly, the police did shoot.

C Winnie Mandela was an eye-witness. From *Part of my Soul* (1985).

The children picked up stones, they used dustbin lids as shields and marched towards machine guns. Children were dying in the street, and as they were dying, the others marched forward, facing guns. The thirst for freedom in children's hearts was such that they were prepared to face those machine guns with stones. That is what happens when you hunger for freedom. Nothing else seems to matter.

We couldn't stop our children. We couldn't keep them off the streets.

D Robert St John saw South African police in action. From *Through Malan's Africa* (1954).

I have seen South African policemen make a baton charge. It is frightening. There is a vicious look in the eyes of most men [making] a baton charge. In the excitement, they become [murderous], perhaps without meaning to.

As the riot spread, so more police and soldiers turned up. Over the next few days, the riots increased. Government buildings, such as beer-halls, were burned down; many cars were destroyed in the streets. The homes of black policemen were attacked.

Vorster instructed the security forces to restore order 'at all costs'. One result was that crowds were fired on without warning, often from the back. The dead included two white men who were pulled from their cars and stoned to death.

E Hector Petersen, aged 13, was the first to die.

F Residents of Soweto drag away a dead man, shot during a demonstration in 1976.

The riots soon spread to other townships. Official figures later stated that 618 people were killed, mostly schoolchildren; another 1500 were injured. Over the next year, nearly 5000 young people under 18 were found guilty of various offences.

In July 1976, the government dropped its plans to introduce teaching in Afrikaans. It held an enquiry into what had happened. The judge decided there was no evidence that communists were to blame. Instead, he blamed the country's apartheid system. It was not what Vorster's government wanted to hear.

As with Sharpeville, the Soweto riots made headline news around the world. But Sharpeville had involved just a few thousand people; in Soweto, tens of thousands had rioted. There was no hope of continuing the policy of détente.

The Soweto riots had other lasting effects. Thousands of blacks fled across the border and joined MK to train as guerrillas. Mandela's wife, Winnie, was banned from Soweto for organising a Black Parents Committee. In later years, there was violence every June on the anniversary of the riots.

'If we do Afrikaans, Vorster must do Zulu' – Soweto protester's slogan

Q

1 a) What caused the Soweto disturbances?
   b) What were the consequences of this event?
2 a) Who do you think was responsible for the violence: the government; the police; the children; the parents; anyone else? Give reasons for your choice(s).
   b) Who was responsible for the deaths? Again, give reasons.

OPPOSITION TO APARTHEID

'Muldergate'

Soweto did not make Vorster unpopular with white voters. In 1977, they gave his Nationalist Party its biggest-ever election victory. However, Vorster resigned in 1978 on the grounds of ill-health and became South African president. He held the job for just eight months before he was forced to retire after the 'Muldergate' scandal was discovered.

This was named after Dr Connie Mulder, the Information Minister, who later resigned. His department had secretly used £30 million of government money on propaganda. It had been spent partly on bribing foreigners to give South Africa a better image abroad. Money had also been spent on making films and publishing a newspaper.

Internal Security Act (1976)

In 1976, all outdoor meetings were banned except sports events and funerals. The Internal Security Act allowed the government to ban any organisation, individual or newspaper. In effect, the Minister of Justice now decided what was a crime and what was not. Suspects were held without trial. But South Africa was a police state long before this happened.

The '90-Day Law'

From 1963 onwards, the police could arrest anyone and hold them in prison for 90 days, on the grounds that they were interrogating them. In 1965, this was extended to 180 days. The police did not need a warrant; they did not need to make a charge; there was no trial.

A Two riot policemen, armed with shotguns, take aim at black youths.

No one knew how many people were locked up and even relatives did not usually know where they were kept. **Detainees** were not allowed visits or legal aid; law courts could not release them. Children under 18 were amongst those locked up.

Under these circumstances, police could treat detainees as brutally as they wished. No one ever visited detainees so only jailers knew if they had black eyes or broken bones. 'Interrogation' often involved torture. Detainees were questioned for days on end, without sleep; they were beaten up or given electrical shock treatment; others were hooded and then partially suffocated.

B Sylvia, a 16-year-old black girl, was detained by police.

> Before you get to your cells, they ask you questions. If you don't understand or don't answer them positively, they just connect some electric wires and they put them through the clothes. You feel shocked and very much pain. Maybe, they put it for two minutes. They repeat the question and, if you don't answer it again, they keep on putting that electric wire on you.

C Khosi Mbatha spoke about her time in jail (1982):

> Some days I'd feel cold steel next to my temple. He would say, 'I'm going to shoot you and nobody will ever know about you because I've got the power and the protection, as a policeman.' Then he walks out, just like that. Some days they would come in and beat me up in the cells.

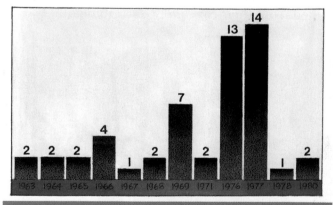

D How many political prisoners died while in police custody, 1963–78.

The first political detainee died in 1963. He had fallen from a twelfth floor window, then a police van had hit him. Causes of death were usually given as 'suicide', 'falling out of a window' and so on. Steve Biko was the most famous black person to die in custody. He had been leader of the all-black South African Students Association (SASO).

SASO was the first black consciousness organisation. These organisations all totally rejected apartheid and refused to work within the system. SASO stressed black self-determination and tried to make black people proud of their history and culture. (The whites always claimed that the blacks had no history worth talking about.)

Biko was against violence and believed that moderate action would bring success. It did not save him or his organisation. In 1973, SASO was banned; in 1977, Biko was arrested and died in detention soon afterwards. It was later reported that Biko died of brain damage as a result of police brutality.

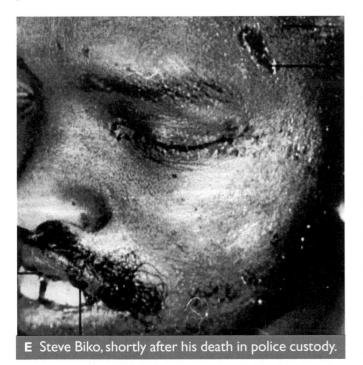

E Steve Biko, shortly after his death in police custody.

Death sentences

None of the government's laws succeeded in reducing violence or opposition to apartheid. In 1979, the government tried a tactic it had not used since the early 1960s – hanging political offenders.

In 1979, Solomon Mahlangu was hanged for working for MK. Other MK members were sentenced to death for treason but campaigns inside and outside South Africa forced the government to think again. The president himself reprieved some of those convicted.

F Boer rock song (1989).

If black and white were one
And policemen just nice,
This country would be
A sweet paradise.

G Mandela and Sisulu in Robben Island jail. This 1966 photograph was the last one of Mandela until 1990.

Nelson Mandela in prison

Meanwhile, Nelson Mandela remained in solitary confinement on Robben Island. His cell was just seven feet square; his bed was a mat on the floor. Light came from one 40 watt light bulb. This was where he spent about 16 hours every day. Every six months, he was allowed to receive and send one letter and have one visit. A jailer was present to make sure that he only talked about family matters.

Over the years, he organised hunger-strikes and go-slows to improve prison conditions. The result was better food, better clothes (long trousers instead of shorts), hot water and more recreation.

In 1973, the Minister of Prisons offered to reduce Mandela's sentence if he would support the idea of the Transkei becoming an 'independent' state. The offer was made a number of times; each time, Mandela refused.

In 1980, the UN Security Council pressed the South African government to release all political prisoners, including Mandela. The government refused but it did improve their prison conditions. From then onwards, they were allowed to read newspapers.

Q

1 a) What could police do under the 90-Day Law?
   b) What are the dangers of imprisonment without trial?
   c) Why was the government able to do things like this?
2 What evidence is there that South Africa (i) was worried about international opinion and (ii) was not? Use both pages for your answer.
3 It is 1979. You are a member of the UN and you oppose apartheid. What can you do about it?

BLACKS AND WHITES

A View of white Johannesburg. Compare this with source A on page 26.

In back garden hidden from road

At least 15 feet from the house

One small window above eye level

B Regulations on accommodation for 'live-in' black servants.

Blacks and whites lived almost separate lives under apartheid. They did not go to school together; they did not live together. If a white person did not want to meet any blacks, they did not have to, except for servants. Some white people knew nothing about pass laws; they never visited black townships.

White South Africans had one of the highest living standards in the world. Many white homes were huge by British standards, with big gardens and a swimming pool. There would often be living quarters for a maid or nanny. Well-off white families employed between one and four servants. Household chores in many white homes were all done by black servants.

White areas had properly-made roads, not dust tracks; there was good street lighting, too. White areas had libraries, museums, public gardens and so on. The whites who ran them could decide when (and if) other races could use them.

However, by 1980, many whites lived in fear in their luxury homes. They kept guard dogs and bought radio equipment to call for help if they were attacked.

Conditions for black workers improved by the early 1980s. Most jobs were opened up to all races but most blacks had poorer education and could not compete with white people for the better jobs. Also, most industries were owned by whites and many chose to employ white workers.

> South African joke: White housewife on telephone: 'I'm sorry but please don't come for morning tea today. One of my maids is ill.'

By contrast, the poor were very poor – and usually black or Coloured. Some of the worst living conditions were in squatter camps. Homes were made of old tins, canvas and wooden boxes. Some families lived there for decades, although police destroyed them from time to time. Toilets were just buckets in iron sheds; they had no roofs; up to five people used them, side by side.

Queues formed at blacks' labour bureaux soon after dawn. Blacks had to present their pass book before they could register for a job. A few whites earned low wages or had no job but most earned good money. There were usually plenty of jobs for whites only.

South Africa offered only limited social security. People without jobs turned to begging or crime. At bus stops or outside restaurants, there were usually black children, begging for money. They spent it on bread and milk, their basic food. Many were orphans with nowhere to live. Whites often swore and spat at them; cold water was thrown over them.

Bad living conditions and a poor diet affected health. In 1978, over 40 per cent of the population had tuberculosis – and no one knew how many cases were not reported. Nearly all those who suffered from it were black; 98 per cent of cases in 1979.

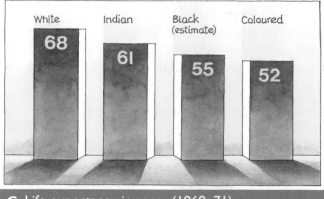

White	Indian	Black (estimate)	Coloured
68	61	55	52

C Life expectancy in years (1969–71).

D The 'Miss Lovely Legs' contest at the supermarket (1980). What might the blacks have thought?

Whites lived longer than blacks not just because they earned more money and had better homes. They also had better health care because health services, like everything else, were segregated. In theory, so was the treatment they received.

In other words, black patients were treated by black doctors and looked after by black nurses in all-black wards. White patients were similarly segregated. However, in 1976, only six out of 693 newly-trained doctors were black. So black patients were often treated by white doctors. On the other hand, there was a shortage of white nurses, so many white patients were cared for by black nurses.

There was little comfort for black people who lived to old age. Outside the bantustans, there were only four black old people's homes, all of them old. The government expected relatives to look after them inside the bantustans but few families could really afford this. Wherever they lived, black pensioners were poorer than white ones.

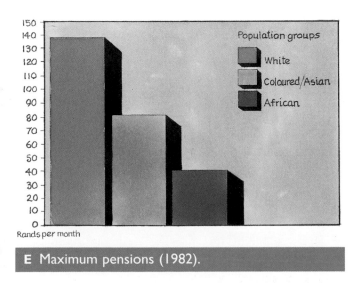

E Maximum pensions (1982).

South African joke: Is making love work or pleasure? 'Pleasure,' says the black man. 'If it was work, the baas would make me do it'

How people felt

F Sureya Dunn, aged 19, was an Asian bank worker (1976).

I took a school trip to Europe and London for a month. When I got back I was very frustrated. We had a lot of freedom there. The other day three friends and I went to a restaurant in Rosebank [a smart white suburb] and the African waiter took our order. Then the white owner sent the waiter back to say he couldn't serve us, but we could take the food away if we wanted. We just left: it was an embarrassment.

G Amanda van Aswegen was an Afrikaner sales girl, aged 17 (1976).

I don't know any blacks of my age, and have never spoken to any. I don't think it is a good idea that black and white should know each other. I would just hate to live with them. I don't like anything about them. I don't know if our [black] maid has any children. I never speak to her. I have never been into a Bantu location and don't want to.

H A black journalist quoted in Anthony Sampson, *Drum* (1956).

It makes me boil having to say "Ya, baas" to a white man who's inferior to me. God, I feel sick when I see an educated African grovelling in front of a white man.

I Anthony Sampson, *Drum* (1956).

'You know, I saw a white woman fall down in the street yesterday,' said Henry [a black man] one morning, 'I was just going up to help her, and then I stopped, and thought: What will the whites think? They'll think I'm trying to rape her. If I pick her up, it means I'll actually have to touch her. A native touching a European woman! Oooh! Terrible! I couldn't risk it, so I walked on.'

J Henry Gibbs, *Twilight in South Africa* (1949).

One [white woman] said to me, 'I have a drop of Native blood, a long way back. I'm not ashamed of it – why should I be? It wasn't my fault – but I daren't admit it. My children and I would be [shunned].

A This British cartoon showed Prime Minister Botha seated on a black man (1986).

In 1978, P W Botha took over from John Vorster as Prime Minister. He realised that apartheid was not working. Some apartheid laws could not be enforced for economic reasons. Sometimes, officials had to turn a blind eye if laws were broken.

For instance, the flow of black workers into the towns could not be stopped because industry needed them. But there was a shortage of skilled workers because Bantu education was so poor. Businessmen needed changes to apartheid. The government knew this and in 1978, the Afrikaner University of Stellenbosch admitted its first non-white students.

Botha came up with a twin policy. On one hand, he used more force to keep the violence under control. On the other, he tried to reform apartheid slowly. But he had no intention of giving it up completely. He rejected the idea of 'one man, one vote' elections.

Botha's reforms

In 1979, black trade unions were made legal. Botha hoped that the government would be able to control them. He was wrong. In 1984, the National Union of Mineworkers called the first legal strike by black miners. They wanted a big pay increase.

Petty apartheid was slowly disappearing. Some public places, such as cinemas, were opened to all. In 1981, beaches in Cape Province stopped being segregated; by 1985, some hotels and restaurants were desegregated, although few non-whites could afford them. However, most facilities remained segregated, including transport, swimming pools and toilets. And reforms were not consistent. For instance, in 1983, Pretoria actually closed 17 parks to black people.

There was political change, too. In 1983, a new **constitution** gave the vote to Indians and Coloureds. However, their representatives could not hold debates with whites; they had separate meetings and whites could veto their decisions. Blacks were still not given the vote.

B The new South African Parliament which opened in 1984.

This new constitution was opposed by a new group called the United Democratic Front (UDF). This brought together about 600 different anti-apartheid organisations. Indians and Coloureds did not like the new system, either. At the 1984 election, over 80 per cent of Indians and Coloureds did not vote.

In 1985, mixed marriages were permitted. However, the Group Areas Act still banned non-whites from living in white areas. This meant that a mixed-race couple could not legally live together. It might also be hard to find a school which would accept their children.

C Protas and Susan Madlala were the first couple to have a legal mixed marriage (1985).

However, the government could no longer enforce the Group Areas Act for economic reasons. By 1986, about 600 000 non-whites needed homes which did not exist in their own areas. Yet there were 37 000 empty houses and flats in white areas. Their white owners were willing to sell to anyone, whatever their colour. By 1986, 25 per cent of residents in three white Johannesburg suburbs were Indian or black.

That year, Botha promised to extend the permit system which allowed blacks and Indians to live in some white suburbs, mainly expensive ones; this was already happening, anyway. In February, Johannesburg's business district was opened up to all races. Yet again, the government had to bow to the needs of business.

D A symptom of petty apartheid from 1977. (Compare this picture to source C on page 38.)

There were other reforms in 1986. Botha abandoned the Pass Laws so all races could come and go freely. However, this did not make it much easier for black people to find jobs and black workers were still paid far less than white people. Finally, blacks were allowed to be full citizens of South Africa. The bantustans had taken away this right.

These reforms did not have the effects which Botha expected. His problem was that he was caught between what different racial groups wanted and his changes satisfied nobody.

Instead, the reforms had two effects. Firstly, non-whites were not satisfied because they wanted apartheid scrapped completely. Violence in the black townships increased and many residents refused to pay their rent. Secondly, the changes caused increased resistance from extreme right-wing whites. Their leader was an ex-policeman, called Eugene Terreblanche. He and his supporters wanted more apartheid, not less. In 1981, the National Party lost support in the general election. In the following year, a new right-wing Conservative Party was launched.

So the government tried a new tactic. In 1984, they tried to get Mandela to help them. They hoped he might condemn the ANC's violence and cause a split in the ANC leadership. The Justice Minister allowed a visit from a British politician.

E Nelson Mandela: *Long Walk to Freedom* (1994).

Professor Dash asked me whether I [was encouraged by] the government's intention of repealing the mixed-marriage laws and certain other apartheid [laws]. 'This is a pinprick,' I said. 'It is not my ambition to marry a white woman or swim in a white pool. It is political equality that we want.'

In January 1985, Botha publicly said that the government would release Mandela if he rejected violence. He added, 'It is not the South African government which now stands in the way of Mr Mandela's freedom. It is he himself.'

F In February, Mandela's daughter, Zindzi, read out his reply at a UDF rally in Soweto:

Only free men can negotiate. Prisoners cannot enter into contracts. I cannot and will not give any undertaking at a time when I and you, the people, are not free. Your freedom and mine cannot be separated. I will return.

G P W Botha described a meeting with black people in *The Sunday Times* (1987).

I was invited to a gathering by the biggest [Church] in South Africa, [mostly] black. In one arena, I addressed more than 3 million people. And they were so well disciplined and well behaved. They were singing hymns, they were praying, but they were also clapping hands while I was speaking.

Q

1 a) Why was it impossible to enforce the Pass Laws?
   b) Why was it impossible to enforce the Group Areas Act?
   c) Why were these two laws a nuisance to businessmen?
2 a) What effects did Botha hope his reforms would have?
   b) What effects did they actually have?
   c) What was the reason for the difference?
3 Read the column above. Was Mandela standing in the way of his own freedom? Explain your answer.

THE MID-80S

Bishop Tutu

One important opponent of apartheid remained free in South Africa. He was Bishop Tutu. As a child, he remembered his black classmates going through dustbins at a nearby white school. They were looking for lunchboxes which the white pupils had thrown away.

A Bishop Tutu speaks out against apartheid in 1986.

In 1975, Tutu became the first black **dean** in the Anglican Church in Johannesburg. He also became general secretary of the South African Council of Churches and bitterly attacked apartheid. He reminded the government that other dictators, like Hitler, had not succeeded.

The government was not pleased when Tutu was awarded the Nobel Peace Prize in 1984. In an opinion poll, 75 per cent of the whites said that he did not deserve the award. But he accepted it on behalf of 'all those people whose noses are rubbed in the dust every day'.

Violence increases

In 1980, white rule ended in Rhodesia. Black people gained the vote and the country was renamed Zimbabwe. This made it easier for the ANC to increase its armed struggle against South Africa. In 1981 alone, it launched over 80 armed attacks. Most of them were against government buildings but some damaged industry. Power stations in Durban were attacked so that white homes and businesses would be affected.

The pressures on Botha were increasing. His white supporters still disagreed about what the government should do. The right-wing wanted firmer action but businessmen wanted more reforms: violence was bad for business.

In the 1980s, Botha used more and more force against the ANC. The South African army invaded nearby countries to attack ANC bases and kill anyone who opposed apartheid. The South African government helped groups fighting against the new governments in Angola and Mozambique. They even took action outside southern Africa. Government agents killed an ANC official in Paris and the ANC's London offices were bombed.

The ANC could not defeat the government in a war. It employed huge, well-armed security forces. The South African Police had 55 000 full-time members, along with another 35 000 part-timers.

So the ANC tried a different tactic. In 1985, Oliver Tambo told people in the townships to make the country **ungovernable.** He wanted non-whites to increase their protests. The ANC believed that this would help to force South Africa to give up apartheid.

Violence had always been a part of township life and it had grown worse in the 1980s. Between September 1984 and January 1986, the security forces killed 628 blacks. During that same period, blacks themselves had killed another 327 blacks, often for **collaborating** with the government.

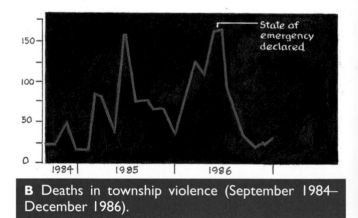

B Deaths in township violence (September 1984–December 1986).

Crossroads (1985)

Crossroads was an illegal squatter town which housed about 100 000 black people, north of Cape Town. Over and over again, police destroyed the shacks and took people 800 miles back to their homelands. But the people walked back again.

In February 1985, Crossroads residents thought they were going to be moved again. So they built barricades of concrete and burning tyres. Black youths threw stones at police and the police fought back with tear gas and rubber bullets. When that did not work, they used shotguns instead: youths then threw petrol bombs. Fighting went on throughout the year, leaving over 1000 blacks dead.

C Violence returns to the community in Crossroads (1985).

The summer of 1985 was especially violent. It was the 25th anniversary of the Sharpeville shootings. In July, the government declared a state of emergency in some urban areas but the protests went on. In November, the government banned foreign cameramen from taking pictures of the 'unrest'.

Half of the violent deaths in 1985 were caused by security forces. In 1986, the pattern of violence changed: more blacks were killed by other blacks than by police. The most common method was to put a car tyre over the victim's head, soak it in petrol and set fire to it. This was known as 'necklacing'. Hundreds died in this way. Law and order was fast disappearing.

Black people had begun to turn on each other. ANC supporters attacked black police and councillors, and burned down their homes. They wanted to make it impossible for the government to control either the townships or the bantustans.

There was also a tribal element in this violence. The leading ANC officials were mostly from the Xhosa tribe; the Zulus had their own organisation, called the Inkatha Freedom Party. Its leader was Chief Buthelezi, a member of the Zulu royal family. ANC and Inkatha supporters were settling their quarrels with guns and sticks.

In June 1986, Botha introduced a new state of emergency which covered the entire country. In September, Bishop Tutu was chosen as the new Archbishop of Cape Town, head of the Anglican Church in South Africa. He was convinced that black victory lay just around the corner.

However, teenagers would pay a price for this victory because they played a major role in the protests. Many young blacks did not attend school for years on end. People called them 'the lost generation'.

> **South African joke:** 'We no longer practise apartheid. We don't need to. We've got it down to a fine art.'

D From a report in *The Sunday Times* (June 1986).

Dan Motsintsi is youth co-ordinator of the United Democratic Front.

He says: 'Today's youth spends 24 hours out of 24 thinking how to rid the country of oppression. It is their full daily occupation. They are organised and determined. The struggle is not just for people's education, but for people's power.'

E Youth unrest at Duduza in 1985.

Q

1 a) What was the ANC's plan?
   b) Was it likely to work? Explain carefully.
   c) What disadvantages did the plan have?
2 a) List all the ways in which teenagers could protest.
   b) Which ones do you think would give the government the biggest problems?
   c) Read source D. What long-term consequences would this have?

ECONOMIC PRESSURE

Black people on their own could not force the government to give in. South Africa's wealth made the government much too powerful. Foreign businesses and governments also had to put pressure on Botha.

In 1985, the American Chase Manhattan Bank refused to continue lending money to South Africa. Other major banks refused to lend more money until the government got rid of apartheid. Over the next two years, dozens of international companies withdrew investments from South Africa. They included Barclays and Esso.

Foreign governments also took action. The British Commonwealth condemned Botha's policies. The USA passed an Anti-Apartheid Act to encourage US firms to take money out of South Africa.

Sanctions

Most countries wanted to use sanctions against South Africa although there was no guarantee that they would work. The British government disagreed. The British Prime Minister, Mrs Thatcher, argued that sanctions would hurt black people more than they would hurt the government.

Some people thought it would be better to invest more money in South Africa because this would make the poorest better-off. They believed that well-off blacks could put more pressure on the government.

In 1986, seven leading Commonwealth politicians visited South Africa to find out whether sanctions would help end apartheid. These seven were called the 'Eminent Persons Group'.

Afterwards, they warned that there would be a bloodbath unless Botha reformed apartheid and talked to the ANC. What they did not know was that talks were secretly taking place. In June 1985, Mandela met Kobie Coetsee, the justice minister, and discussed the way forward.

In 1986, foreign governments began to take firm action. Both the USA and the EEC imposed new sanctions against South Africa. They had two effects. First, they cost South Africa millions of pounds over the next few years. Second, black unemployment in the townships doubled. By 1987, 25 per cent of black workers had no job. This helped the ANC to recruit new members.

However, it would still take a long time for sanctions alone to defeat the white government. South Africa had rich farming land and plenty of raw materials. It could produce almost everything it needed. In any case, other nations needed its products. South Africa exported coal, iron and steel, as well as diamonds and gold. South Africa supplied over half the world's gold; each year, it supplied nearly half the world's platinum.

Sanctions did not bring a sudden end to apartheid. This was partly because the sanctions did not cover everything and partly because too many companies found ways round the laws and went on trading.

A A protest march in London calling for sanctions against South Africa.

CHANGE **WILL** COME TO SOUTH AFRICA – BUT NOT UNTIL WE SAY SO

ROGER BEALE

B A British cartoon from March 1988. The white man is President Botha.

C *The Times* described what happened to a black couple in 1987.

Mr Robert Mnculwana and his wife Elka were arrested last Sunday in a park in Germiston. [They were] kept overnight in a police cell and given a choice between a month in jail or paying a fine of £30 each.

A police spokesman said that the police had acted in response to a complaint that blacks were sitting in a whites-only park. 'There is a large sign which states that the park is reserved for whites,' he explained.

President Botha had said that petty apartheid was 'outdated' but stories like this proved that it went on. They added to international complaints against South Africa. In 1987, the National Party won another big victory in the General Election. The right-wing Conservative Party also did well: they wanted the government to be stricter with the blacks.

In May 1988, the United Nations again demanded the release of Nelson Mandela. In July, he celebrated his 70th birthday. A huge concert was held at Wembley Stadium and was broadcast around the world. A billion television viewers did not know that apartheid would soon be gone for good.

Did apartheid benefit blacks?

F Some blacks had become wealthy. Maud Motanyane was one of them. She edited a magazine, aimed at young blacks.

D Dr C Mulder: *Progress Through Separate Development*, published in 1973 by the South African Government.

Very few countries can equal South Africa's high standard of living for all its peoples, comparatively speaking. Maybe that is why we have checkpoints on our borders to prevent people from illegally entering South Africa to find employment and a higher standard of living. I have never heard of free people [willingly] trying to slip into a police state (as South Africa is often made out to be).

G In 1988, Maud Motanyane told the *Sunday Times*:

With wealth you speak from a position of strength but it doesn't insulate you from the system. When someone rich [and black] walks down the street, to almost any white he is just another kaffir.

E Total income in rands (after paying taxes, rent, etc). From a South African government advertisement (1989).

	Whites	Blacks
1970	33.3	15.9
1985	40.0	32.1
2000 (estimate)	44.2	53.6

Q

1 a) Why were sanctions introduced?
   b) Why was it difficult to make sanctions work against South Africa?
   c) What point did the cartoonist make in source B?
2 Read the column on the right.
   a) Why should you be careful about sources D and E?
   b) Does source D prove that blacks did not object to apartheid?
   c) Read source G and think carefully. How had white attitudes changed since 1948?

The End of Apartheid

In June 1987, Botha declared a new state of emergency. The ANC had wanted to make the country ungovernable and it was succeeding. The violence was a key issue in talks between the government and the ANC. The government had always said that it would not talk to organisations which used violence. So it wanted the ANC to end the violence before public talks began. Mandela refused. He claimed that the violence was being caused by government policies.

In August 1988, Mandela had an emergency operation for tuberculosis and was later moved to a cottage at Victor Verster prison near Cape Town. The justice minister brought him a case of wine as a house-warming present! He also told Mandela that it would be his last home before becoming a free man. It was a comfortable place where the talks could go on.

Botha needed the talks to succeed because sanctions were hurting industry and the townships were out of control. But the talks had not got far when, in January 1989, Botha suffered a stroke. The following month, he resigned as National Party leader but stayed on as South African president.

A In March, Mandela wrote to Botha:

> **I am disturbed as many other South Africans no doubt are, by the *spectre* of a South Africa split into two hostile camps – blacks on one side and whites on the other, slaughtering one another.**

Botha and Mandela had a brief meeting in July (source B) but no decisions were made. In August, Botha resigned as president and F W De Klerk took over. De Klerk was an Afrikaner who did not believe in majority rule, any more than Botha did.

B Petty apartheid! (1985.)

However, de Klerk realised that new policies were needed. At the General Election in September 1989, he promised that apartheid would be reformed. Just days later, Cape Town had its biggest anti-apartheid march in 30 years. De Klerk could have banned it but he let it go ahead.

Other actions suggested that De Klerk would prove to be different to Botha. In October, he released Walter Sisulu and some other black prisoners. He began to demolish petty apartheid. Beaches were opened to people of all races and he announced that the Separate Amenities Act would be repealed. This law had segregated public places, such as parks.

C The breakdown of petty apartheid (1991).

In December, De Klerk met Mandela, who asked him to lift the ban on the ANC. The cabinet agreed to do this. They may have thought that the ANC did not offer a major threat at that moment. The ANC's organisation was weak and revolutions in eastern Europe had caused communism to collapse.

D On February 2 1990, De Klerk told Parliament that:

- the bans on the ANC and PAC were ended, along with bans on over 30 other organisations
- political prisoners who had not committed violent crimes would be released
- newspapers could report events freely
- the death sentence would be stopped
- Mandela would be released, without conditions

I don't care if there is a black government, as long as I can get back to proper police work. I'm tired of defending apartheid laws for the sake of politicians. I don't care who lives next door to me as long as they don't disturb my life.

De Klerk also said that 'the time for negotiation has arrived'. But some white politicians booed when de Klerk announced the changes.

On February 11, Mandela was released from Victor Verster prison. He was free for the first time in 27 years. A crowd of 2000 watched him leave. He told them: 'I greet you in the name of peace, democracy and freedom for all'.

F Free at last: Mandela (centre) celebrated with his wife Winnie and Walter Sisulu.

G Soon afterwards, Mandela told 100 000 ANC supporters at Soweto soccer stadium:

Your strength, your discipline, has released me to stand before you today. It's not just the kings and generals who make history; it is the people, the masses, workers, peasants, doctors, clergy, all our people! I have seen them make history and that is why all of us are here today.

De Klerk had hoped that Mandela would ask for sanctions to end; he did not. De Klerk had hoped that Mandela would condemn the violence; he did not. Mandela's release did not solve the government's problems, as De Klerk had expected.

Both the ANC and the government wanted talks because each needed to show its supporters that its policy was working. The government wanted the violence to stop and the ANC wanted the government to end apartheid and the state of emergency.

Coloured diner to a Coloured waiter: 'Have you got some ice cream?' Waiter: 'Yes. Ice cream, chocolate sauce and some nuts. That's our South Africa problem.' (1986)

There was one basic disagreement at these talks. The ANC wanted a constitution which gave every adult a vote; this would guarantee black majority rule. De Klerk wanted a system in which power was shared and whites could veto black laws. This would prevent majority rule.

Formal talks began in May in Cape Town. It was the first official meeting between the two sides and talks went well. They agreed to work together to end the violence and reach a political settlement. Two days later, P W Botha resigned from the National Party in protest.

H The two sides issued the Groote Schuur Minute (May 1990). They agreed:

- **to end the state of emergency (except in Natal, where violence was worst)**
- **to set up a joint working group to negotiate peacefully**

In June, Mandela set off on a tour of Europe and North America. While he was away, the government ended the state of emergency, except in Natal. In August, the two sides signed the Pretoria Minute.

I The Pretoria Minute (August 1990).

- **The ANC would suspend its armed struggle.**
- **The government would review the Internal Security Act.**
- **Dates were set for the release of political prisoners.**

Q

1 a) Why did the government want talks?
  b) Why did the ANC want talks?
  c) What issues did they disagree about?
2 Mandela refused to give renounce violence before talks started. The government refused to start talks until he had done this. Why, in the end, did the government give in?
3 Who do you think had the upper hand by 1990? Give reasons.

INKATHA VERSUS THE ANC

A Other blacks attacked this Zulu because they thought he was an Inkatha spy.

B The South African *Sunday Star* reported the event (1990).

A group armed with *machetes* and crude spears questioned people getting off a train. Suddenly, they began pushing a large man down the stairs towards the street.

Attackers kicked the man, then hit him with fist-sized stones. Several plunged small daggers into his back and chest. They kicked him down and some hurled boulders at his head. More rocks hit him and he collapsed. Someone poured petrol on him. When the match struck, he burst into flames and leaped in the air. Onlookers yelled what sounded like a cheer. A woman danced.

C The final moments.

The Inkatha Freedom Party

The ANC ended its armed struggle but South Africa did not become more peaceful; in fact, it became more violent. The worst violence occurred in Natal, where Inkatha was based. War between ANC and Inkatha had killed 3000 people in the previous three years. (This was more than had died in Northern Ireland in the previous 20 years.)

Chief Buthelezi, Prime Minister of KwaZulu, was not popular with ANC members because he had criticised ANC violence and he had opposed sanctions. However, the ANC could not ignore Buthelezi because he was a leading black politician.

The government allowed Zulus to carry their traditional tribal weapons when they held meetings (source D). The ANC believed this helped to cause the violence.

The ANC also thought there was something odd about some Inkatha attacks. For instance, about 30 people were hacked to death when busloads of armed Inkatha members entered Sebokeng township. They had had a police escort. Later in 1990, Inkatha supporters drove ANC supporters out of Zonkizizwe squatter camp and took their property. Once again, the police had escorted them.

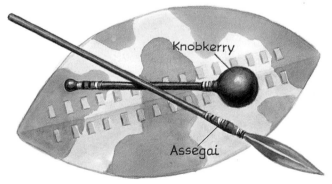

D An artist's impression of two traditional Zulu weapons.

The 'Third Force'

In September 1990, Mandela claimed that an unknown 'Third Force' was causing conflict between the ANC and Inkatha. He believed that they were men from the security services who wanted to disrupt the talks. Mandela thought the attacks were organised by the government. The government claimed it knew nothing about this 'Third Force'.

"We the judge, the jury, the investigating officer, the prosecutor, and the accused, find us not guilty."

E *Sunday Star* cartoon about police corruption.

The ANC suspected that the security forces helped Inkatha, hoping to start a black civil war. This would have allowed the government to call off talks. However, the government itself claimed that the violence was caused by migrant hostel workers in the townships. They said it was purely tribal – Zulus against Xhosas.

Many attacks had two things in common. First, they were launched by Inkatha supporters. Second, the police did nothing to stop them or seemed to help them. The result was that they made it difficult for the ANC to get organised, especially in Natal.

Over 3500 people died in South Africa in 1990. It was the second most dangerous country on earth. In 1991, the ANC and Inkatha signed a peace agreement but it did not improve the situation, nor did complaints to the government.

In April, Mandela wrote to De Klerk. He pointed out that the attacks were all similar. The police never arrested the murderers; in fact, sometimes, the army or police added to the violence. Also, the violence usually happened just when the ANC was launching a campaign.

The police and Inkatha

Eventually, Mandela was proved right. There was a third force. In 1991, it was revealed that the police Security Branch had been helping Inkatha by giving them large sums of money. The government claimed this was to pay for Inkatha rallies because Inkatha was opposed to sanctions.
But this was not the whole story. It was later revealed that, back in 1986, 200 Inkatha men had been secretly trained by the South African army to use explosives and firearms. These men later became police in KwaZulu. They went on to form hit squads to attack ANC communications across the country.

This had two main effects. It weakened the ANC and made it hard for it to get organised for elections. It also gave the impression that blacks were not fit to rule South Africa.

Beginning in 1989, a secret branch of the South African police trained Zulu hit squads and supplied them with arms. They even helped plan the massacres. They also carried out random killings on commuter trains. Senior officers were aware of this.

Police corruption

Evidence gradually emerged which proved that the police had not always obeyed the law themselves. In the 1980s, police crimes were covered up. But, in 1992, a police captain was sentenced to death for ordering the death of eleven blacks in 1988.

That same year, a doctor who had carried out police **autopsies** claimed that 200 people had been killed in police custody in the previous six years. He alleged that 'the lower rungs of the police are totally out of control'. The government ordered an investigation.

Q

1 a) Explain the role played by the police and army in encouraging violence.
  b) Why did some whites want to encourage the violence?
2 a) Why was black violence a problem for the ANC?
  b) Why was black violence a problem for de Klerk?
  c) How did it help de Klerk?
3 What point is the cartoonist making in source E? Explain your answer fully.

THE BUILD-UP TO THE ELECTION

CODESA

A De Klerk's reforms and the world's responses.	
March 1990:	Namibia gained independence from South Africa
October 1990:	Separate Amenities Act repealed
	National Party allowed people of all races to become members
June 1991:	Group Areas Act repealed
International Reactions:	
April 1991:	EC decided to end sanctions
July:	USA ended sanctions
	Cricket boycott ended and South Africa allowed back into the Olympics

Despite the violence, there was progress. In February 1991, de Klerk announced that the last apartheid laws would be scrapped. This brought cries of 'traitor' from white extremists, especially the **AWB**.

In December, politicians of all races attended the first meeting of the Convention for a Democratic South Africa (CODESA). The convention's job was to work out a new constitution and plan how to govern South Africa in the meantime. Right-wing whites boycotted the talks; so did the PAC, which said the talks were a sell-out to whites. Its slogan was 'One settler, one bullet'.

B Sign of the times: a mixed-race primary school (1992).

The white referendum

The ANC and the government quickly agreed on arrangements for an **interim** government and a General Election, with votes for all. But there was one major disagreement. De Klerk wanted to see 'checks and balances' built into the constitution. In effect, it was another way of getting a white veto.

Some whites criticised the government's reforms so de Klerk held a referendum in March 1992. All white voters were asked whether they supported the reform process and the talks on a new constitution. Nearly 70 per cent of voters said 'Yes'. De Klerk told cheering supporters, 'Today, we have closed the book on apartheid.'

ANC pressure

In June 1992, 42 people were shot or hacked to death at Boipatong squatter camp. Squatters said that police trucks had brought alleged Inkatha supporters to the camp. Inkatha made other attacks that month. As before, no one was arrested for the killings.

The ANC broke off the talks in protest. Along with trade unions and the Communist Party, it began a mass campaign to show the government how much support it had. There were demonstrations and a two-day national strike in August. Four million people stopped work and much of the nation came to a standstill.

In September, during an ANC march in Ciskei homeland, local troops killed 28 and wounded over 200. The ANC was furious. It seemed as if the talks had reached a complete deadlock. Then, de Klerk and Mandela held a summit meeting to try to settle their differences.

C Mandela and de Klerk signed a Record of Understanding (September 1992). They agreed that:
1 An elected assembly would draft a new constitution.
2 They would set up an interim government.
3 An independent group would study police actions.
4 Hostels would be fenced in, to protect inmates.
5 Zulu 'traditional weapons' would be banned at rallies.

This time, Chief Buthelezi was angry. He said that de Klerk had betrayed him and he broke off relations. Fencing in hostels, he said, was like creating Zulu concentration camps.

Power-sharing agreement

An agreement was finally reached in February 1993. There would be an election in which every adult could vote. Any party which achieved 5 per cent of the total vote would be represented in the new **cabinet.** Afterwards, whites would share power in a new government of national unity for five years.

This agreement offered protection for anxious whites. The compromise was first suggested by the South African Communist Party. Two months later, its leader, Chris Hani, was assassinated by a white right-winger.

D The body of Chris Hani, draped by an ANC flag (1993).

Election date set

Reaching an agreement had become urgent. It seemed the only way of controlling the violence. But South Africa also faced other, huge problems. About half the workforce (mostly black) was out of work. About 3 million of them were uneducated youths of the 'lost generation'. The economy had slumped so no new jobs were being created.

In June, the two sides at last set a date for the country's first democratic election – 27 April 1994. This did not please everybody. Chief Buthelezi and the Conservative Party walked out of the talks.

Inkatha's involvement was important. KwaZulu was only a small homeland but nearly a quarter of all South Africans lived there. The 8.5 million Zulus were South Africa's largest tribe. The ANC could win the election on its own. But, without Zulu support, it could not unite the nation. There was even a risk that KwaZulu might declare independence.

E When blacks were allowed to live in white areas, they flooded into Johannesburg. But houses were scarce. This girl's family lived in a garbage dump.

F *The Sunday Times* reported (1993):

Alatta Macuthwana has spent the past four months living with her husband and baby in a pigsty. Nothing, she thought, could get worse. Then, last week, it did: she was threatened with eviction.

The Macuthwanas share the disused pigsties, on the outskirts of Johannesburg, with 22 other black families. Each pays £10 a month to a white farmer.

[He did not] bother to install toilets or running water. He left it to his tenants to clear up and build walls and roofs. Flies, attracted by the manure nearby, plague the eyes of toddlers playing in the dirt. The 60 pigsty dwellers share a hole in the ground as a toilet.

It is because of these health hazards that the authorities last week threatened eviction.

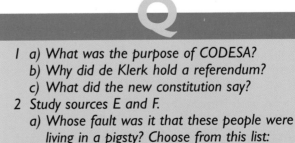

1 a) What was the purpose of CODESA?
   b) Why did de Klerk hold a referendum?
   c) What did the new constitution say?
2 Study sources E and F.
   a) Whose fault was it that these people were living in a pigsty? Choose from this list: Dr Malan; Dr Verwoerd; Mr de Klerk; the farmer; Mandela; themselves. (You may choose others if you wish.) Give reasons for your choices.
   b) What do you think these people wanted from a black government? (Think carefully.)

WHITE RULE ENDS

A A British cartoon of 1993.

In December 1993, over 300 years of white rule ended. A Transitional Executive Council (TEC) was set up to run the country until the election. Blacks had a share in government for the first time. That same month, the bantustans were officially scrapped.

Yet the Zulu boycott continued. Chief Buthelezi still insisted on KwaZulu running its own affairs. Right-wing whites were also demanding their own Afrikaner homeland and threatening war if they did not get it. Neither Inkatha nor the Conservative Party registered to take part in the election.

Mandela knew that the ANC would win the election. But he needed to stop the violence. If he did not, rich whites might leave South Africa, taking their wealth with them; foreign firms might not want to invest. So, in February 1994, the sides held more talks and Mandela made **concessions**: local councils were given more powers and the Zulus were allowed some self-determination.

President Mangope, the ruler of Bophuthatswana bantustan, did not want to take part, either. He did not wish to be part of a united South Africa. However, most of his people disagreed with him and there was an uprising. Students fought running battles with the bantustan police. Strikes hit the civil service and the TV network. In March, Mangope was overthrown and South Africa took over the bantustan.

Also in March, an Inkatha march through Johannesburg ended in violence. Fifty three people died when they tried to force a way into the ANC HQ. Zulu youths later complained to the police that they had been imprisoned and tortured by ANC security guards in the same building.

Inkatha wanted to postpone the election but the other political parties refused. Buthelezi wanted the Zulu kingdom restored and threatened to break away from South Africa. Violence grew so bad in Natal that a new state of emergency was declared in April. In the final days, Buthelezi agreed to let Inkatha join in the elections after promises that the Zulu monarchy would continue.

The election (April 1994)

For the first time, 16 million black people were allowed to vote. About half of them could not read. They were given a voting slip which offered them 19 parties to choose from. Each party was shown by its official logo, its name and a photograph of the party leader.

In rural areas, voters walked up to 60 miles to cast their vote. People feared riots in the townships, if people had to wait too long. In fact, white and black patiently waited in line, sometimes for hours. The election went peacefully.

The ANC won the election easily, gaining 62 per cent of the vote. The National Party polled 20 per cent, with Inkatha winning 10 per cent, although Inkatha won more votes than the ANC in KwaZulu. The ANC's campaign of violence had helped it. Back in 1977, more people had supported Inkatha than the ANC.

B Sign of the times. The first black Miss South Africa in this photograph was only the second black person to speak at an all-white club (1994).

If the ANC had won 66 per cent of the vote, they could have changed the constitution at once. Instead, they would have to wait until 1999 before they could make changes. Secretly, leading ANC officials were pleased. They wanted whites in the government so they could later blame them for anything that went wrong.

In May, Mandela became president, with de Klerk as second deputy president. Two national anthems were played – 'Die Stem', the old Afrikaner one, and 'Nkosi Sikelel' i Afrika', the new one.

D The new South African national anthem (a Xhosa protest song).

Gold bless Africa,	Come spirit
Let her fame resound.	(Come spirit come)
Hear our prayers	Come spirit
God bless	(Come spirit come)
We are her people.	Come holy spirit
	God bless
	We are her people.

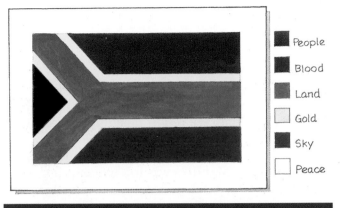

People
Blood
Land
Gold
Sky
Peace

F The new South African flag, which includes the ANC colours.

The government may have looked united but it was not. Inkatha did not wish to play a full role in the new South Africa, nor did right-wing whites. Also, it would be difficult for Mandela to please his communist supporters and keep the support of rich blacks.

However, there were hopeful signs. Most of the population wanted an end to violence: they needed the new government to be successful. Mandela himself was respected by most blacks and whites. And the ANC was not a new political party: it had existed for over 80 years.

Above all, South Africa was richer than most other African countries. The government would need this wealth to provide new houses, better education and more health care. Millions of poor blacks expected great things of their new leader.

In 1994, 18 million black families earned less than £150 per month. Half of the black population could not read or write. Half of the black workforce had no job.

E Mandela (right), de Klerk (centre) and Chief Buthelezi (left) shake hands at the start of a new era.

Q

1 Mandela said, 'I don't think there is much history can say about me.' Do you agree? Explain your answer in detail.
2 Look at the voting figures. How do they suggest that a united South Africa was going to be hard to achieve?
3 a) Look at source B. What feelings do you think Verwoerd would have had about this picture?
   b) What might Mandela have thought?
   c) What might poor blacks have thought?
4 Imagine you are Mandela at this point. What policies would be your priorities in 1994? Explain how you decided.

13

After Apartheid

In 1994, South Africa rejoined the United Nations and the Commonwealth. Apartheid was over. But repairing the damage might take 50 years – about as long as the apartheid era itself. The new government gave more jobs to blacks but some blacks thought Mandela was too easy on the whites. The first black government certainly had plenty to sort out.

One problem was finding out what crimes former governments had committed. Many whites had secrets to hide. In early 1994, whites gave a secret **amnesty** to 3500 police for crimes against blacks. President Mandela later set up a commission to look into crimes committed under apartheid and decide who should be let off. He hoped this would help people forget about the past.

By mid-1995, over 2000 people had admitted to dirty tricks under apartheid. They included police, soldiers and government officials. Proving crimes might be difficult because many records had been destroyed. But some people were tracked down. Police discovered a secret police death squad and one ex-policeman was charged with nine murders.

Mandela quickly corrected another of apartheid's wrongs. Between 1960 and 1990, 3.5 million people were forced to leave their homes. Most of them were black. In 1994, they were offered the chance to get their old lands back. The aim was to give back 30 per cent of South Africa's farming land by 1999.

B Sign of the future? This child belonged to the right-wing AWB. It still demanded a white homeland.

The cost of change

Money was one major problem. Experts reckoned that sanctions had cost South Africa about $27 billions. Lack of investment meant jobs were lost; people without jobs turned to crime. South Africa did not suddenly become peaceful in 1994: you were six times more likely to be murdered in South Africa than in the USA. Many ANC supporters refused to turn in their guns. One young black said bitterly, 'The same old whites are in control.'

The USA offered aid in 1994 and investors poured money into South Africa. But billions of pounds were needed. Most blacks did not have clean water, rubbish collection, sewers or paved streets.

C Some of South Africa's problems (1995).
(Total population: 50 millions)
2 million black children were not in school.
2 million people suffered from malnutrition.
3 million homes were needed.
8 million people lived in squatter camps.
10 million people had no drinking water at home.
15 million had no toilet.
23 million had no electricity.

Making the money to pay for these was a problem in itself. Most black workers had too little education; millions of children in the 'lost generation' had none at all. Two-thirds of black pupils did not finish their education. Those who did mostly failed their final exams.

A The Pedi people returned to land they lost in 1974 in return for £6 compensation (1994).

The Zulus

The Zulus were the second big problem. Chief Buthelezi drew up plans for a semi-independent homeland inside South Africa; he did not believe that a centralised South Africa would work. The ANC was determined to prove him wrong. But Inkatha walked out of talks about a new South African constitution.

Mandela knew he could not ignore the Zulus. If Buthelezi declared KwaZulu independent, it would lead to a civil war. That would be a disaster. Industry would stop investing and jobs would be lost. The government would not be able to afford to improve living conditions.

Meanwhile, police were investigating hundreds of murders going back ten years in KwaZulu-Natal. In 1995, three members of a 'Third Force' hit-squad were sent to prison for a total of 202 years. In the early 1990s, they had killed ANC supporters. Many people thought that the 'Third Force' was still operating, with police turning a blind eye.

Over a year after the election, two people a day were being killed in KwaZulu-Natal. Arguments between the ANC and Inkatha were as fierce as ever. Many whites thought that the Zulus and Xhosas could never live together peacefully. And, as a senior Inkatha leader said, 'Remember you can't ignore the Zulu people'.

D Buthelezi told a Zulu rally what he thought of the ANC (1995).

> To be ignored as if we are no more than just scum, is worse than the [scorn] with which we were treated by racist [governments] for so long.

E Sign of the future? Buthelezi (left) and the Zulu king at a Zulu rally (1992).

F Symbol of the past? There were once 500 000 San (Bushmen); now, there are only 30 000. These ones lived on a game reserve, in return for posing for tourists.

G *Time* magazine (May 1995).

> A year of freedom has filled blacks and whites alike with pride and, most important, hope.
>
> Yes, it is true that Mandela's government has so far built fewer than 1000 of the 1 million houses it promised to construct in five years. It is also true that the unemployment rate among blacks remains at 41 per cent and that the whites still own 75 per cent of the land, although they make up only 13 per cent of the population.

Much of the success was due to President Mandela himself. He trod a careful course between improving life for the blacks and not upsetting white business leaders. South Africa's economy was still mainly controlled by whites – and it will stay that way well into the 21st century.

A 1995 opinion poll showed that 55 per cent of whites thought Mandela was doing a good job. Blacks showed their support in many small ways. Before the election, 80 per cent of Soweto residents refused to pay their electricity bills; a year later, only just over 30 per cent were still not paying.

Health care was made free for all young children and pregnant women. More than five million school pupils were given a free peanut-butter sandwich for lunch every day. It provided 25 per cent of the nutrition they needed. The children called them Mandela sandwiches.

In 1995, South Africa's Springbok rugby team won the World Cup. Mandela presented the cup to captain Francois Pienaar. 'Thank you,' he said, 'for what you have done for South Africa.' Pienaar replied, 'We could never do what you have done for South Africa.'

Most South Africans would have agreed.

Afterword

Bram Fischer, who led the defence in the Treason Trial, later gave up his legal work. He died in jail in 1977.

Anton Lembede died suddenly in 1947 after developing an intestinal problem at lunchtime. He died in hospital on the same day.

Chief Luthuli was found dead beside a railway track in 1967, having been hit by a train. He was on a route which he had walked on many occasions.

Nelson Mandela and F W de Klerk were jointly awarded the Nobel Peace Prize in 1993.

Winnie Mandela was sentenced on charges of kidnap and assault in 1990 and fined £3000. She and her husband separated in 1992. In 1995, he sacked her from her job as deputy minister for criticising the government. He later announced that they were divorcing.

Namibia became independent in 1990. It was the last African colony to do so.

Orania is a whites-only town on the Orange River, set up by Dr Verwoerd's son-in-law in 1991. In 1995, Mandela travelled there to meet Mrs Verwoerd, Dr Verwoerd's widow.

Eschel Rhoodie, who masterminded South Africa's secret propaganda campaign in the 1970s, died in 1993. Revelations about Rhoodie's use of secret funds led to the resignation of John Vorster.

After serving his three-year prison sentence, Robert Sobukwe was kept in Robben Island jail until 1969. He was then confined in Kimberley under a banning order and died there in 1978.

Jan Smuts died in 1950.

Oliver Tambo died in 1993.

A state funeral was held for Dr Verwoerd in the Union Buildings in Pretoria. His murderer claimed that a giant tape worm inside his body forced him to commit the murder. He was found to be insane.

John Vorster died in 1983.

Glossary

abstained – did not vote
amnesty – pardon for crimes
assassinated – murdered
autopsies – examinations of dead bodies
AWB – Afrikaans Resistance Movement (an extreme right-wing white group)
bioscope – cinema
boycotted – refused to have anything to do with
cabinet – group of ministers who run a country
civil disobedience – peaceful refusal to obey laws
collaborating – working with
commission – group of people chosen to study something
concentration camp – camp where one group held its enemies
concessions – rights granted
constitution – written rules for running a country
dean – senior clergyman
defiance – resistance to the government
detainee – person held in custody
détente – relaxing of tension
democracy – country in which everyone may vote
domination – control

forefathers – ancestors
immigration – coming into a country to live
integration – bringing together (different races)
interim – for the time being
machete – broad, heavy knife
mandate – right to govern another country
migrant – moving from one place to another
militant – fighting; warlike
minister – serve
propaganda – attempts to persuade people to believe something
referendum – vote by people on a single issue
reservation – land reserved (for living in)
resolution – decision
sabotage – deliberate destruction
sanctions – penalties
segregation – situation in which different racial groups are separated
spectre – ghost
squatting – living on someone else's land
ungovernable – impossible to control
veto – the power to say 'no'
white supremacy – whites in power over blacks